OKAVANGO ADVENTURE

In Search of Animals in Southern Africa

JEREMY MALLINSON

Foreword by Gerald Durrell

David & Charles: Newton Abbot

0 7153 6259 3

Set in Linotype 11/13 Pilgrim
and printed in Great Britain
by John Sherratt and Son Ltd
at the St Ann's Press Park Road Altrincham
for David & Charles (Holdings) Limited
South Devon House Newton Abbot Devon

In fondest memory
of
Tissi and Gub

Contents

CONTENTS

Illustrations

ILLUSTRATIONS

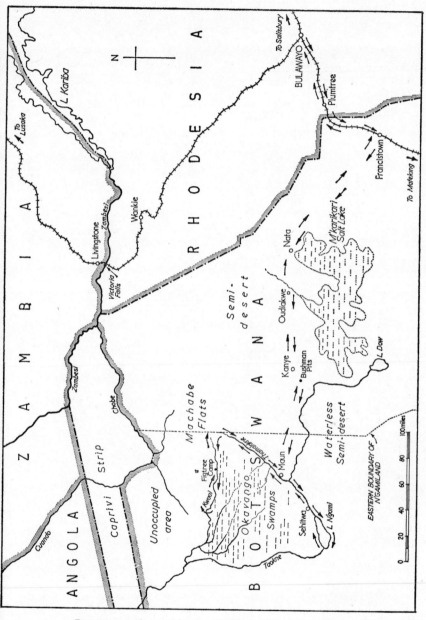

Botswana, the territory of *Okavango Adventure*

Foreword

IN case anyone should think differently, let me put it on record that I had the greatest difficulty in persuading the author of the book to allow me to write this introduction, so modest is he of his achievement.

This is really a most refreshing and enchanting book. It is that very rare species, a travel-animal book that makes you laugh, for never for a moment does the author take himself too seriously and he has avoided all the pomposity that besets nearly everyone when they start to write up their 'experiences'.

Jeremy Mallinson spikes the story of his adventures with some most endearing self-mockery, but at the same time his obvious concern for and love of animal life shine from his prose. This is the story of a great achievement, for the author, being, as he admits, as green as a baby asparagus when it came to animal collecting, nevertheless organised his trip himself (in itself no mean feat, as I know) and then after many adventures and mistakes – and how *nice* to read a book with the mistakes enumerated and not glossed over – he triumphantly returned with a lovely collection of animals.

Everyone yearning for an animal-collecting career (and if my mail is anything to go by, this includes the entire population of Great Britain) should read, digest and learn from this book. For one can learn from it – everything from the difficulties of force-feeding a kingfisher to attending to the internal wants of a constipated lion. This last, of course, is invaluable information for, as Jeremy Mallinson sagely points out, 'it is not as easy as you might think to give a male lion an enema'.

It will be obvious from this book that all animal life has a staunch, honest and loyal friend in Jeremy Mallinson. I wish there were a few more people like him in the world.

GERALD DURRELL

CHAPTER I

Animal Flirtation

ON a cold October afternoon I sailed from Tilbury; and began the considerable adventure of an animal-gathering tour of Africa.

Nowadays, of course, a tour of this kind is rather less adventurous than it would have been in the great days of nineteenth-century exploration. But my grandmother, a child of the Victorian age, seemed to think that Africa had changed little since the days of Dr Livingstone: she wrote in great anxiety, warning me against tropical diseases and urging me to take plenty of disinfectants. Her fears were exaggerated: even so, the voyage very nearly did begin with disaster. I had been in touch with the zoo at Pretoria, and had agreed to take them out a pair of European red foxes. The dog fox gave no trouble: I collected him from the Jersey Zoo, where he had outgrown his quarters. But I had to advertise for a vixen, and eventually bought one from some people in Pembrokeshire: she was sent by train, and arrived at Euston so very late that I nearly missed the boat train for Tilbury.

Exhilarated by this hair's breadth escape, I stood on deck as the Union Castle liner pulled away from the dockside and moved off down the Thames estuary, round into the Channel, and on towards the east coast of Africa and eventually to Capetown.

I had an impressive collection of baggage with me. There were collapsible wire cages, and traps, and nets; there was a Red Cross box for emergencies; there were trunks and suitcases, overdue for retirement but sentimentally cherished; there was a typewriter and a tape-recorder. I disposed things as well as I could, lodging my two foxes on the aft upper deck, where a smell like that of a foxes' earth soon began to prevail: this distressed the domestic canines that were also lodged there, but it had the advantage of keeping nosey people at a distance. I soon found that I had to look after my two foxes myself. In theory a member of the crew – curiously called the 'lamp-trimmer' – was supposed to feed all the livestock on board; but he was not allowed to take the foxes out, and he was too timid to clean the kennels out properly when they were occupied. His answer to this problem was to deep-litter them so lavishly that they could hardly stand up. But I had very little trouble. The dog fox was a little aloof and unapproachable; but the vixen, whom I named Pufelli, was very tame and wagged her tail whenever I came near.

Soon we put in at Gibraltar, our first port of call. I went ashore and visited Prince Ferdinand's Battery on the rock to see the famous apes: there are about thirty-five of them. Barbary apes, and apart from *homo sapiens*, they are the only primates to be found in Europe. I found them an entertaining sight: peering about them from under the heavy prominent brows that protect their eyes from the fierce winds of the Rock, they reminded me of so many sea captains, scanning nautical horizons from under peaked caps. The greyish-brown adults would pester visitors for food, while the black-furred infants developed the arts of mischief to a high degree of perfection.

I went back to the town and astonished the shopkeepers with a problem rather unusual among souvenir-hunting tourists: I needed some wood-wool. This aroused a good deal of curiosity, and I explained that I needed it to provide extra bedding for my foxes on the *Warwick Castle*, since they had suffered a rough time in the Bay of Biscay. The fourth shop that I tried was able to oblige, and I returned to the ship with a huge sack of the stuff on my shoulder, looking rather as though I had been buying tax-free luxury goods in quantity.

We resumed our voyage, and as we cruised through the

Lions: (*above*) Timmy, the dwarf lion; (*below*) Chinky, 'What is that photographer's name?'

(*above*) 'Chinky, you are a messy drinker, don't deny it!' (*below*)
Self, Chinky, my father. My only picture of Chinky showing her
great size. My father happened to be 'in town'.

Mediterranean, I persuaded the First Officer to let me exercise Pufelli along the passenger deck. He was intrigued. 'First time I've seen one of those damned animals so close,' he said, 'usually they're all torn to shreds by the time I catch up with the hounds.' Pufelli flattened her ears and curled her lips in a snarl, as if recognising an enemy of her species. 'Beautiful animals, really, when you get a close look at them,' the First Officer went on; and added defensively, 'You've got to remember that if they weren't preserved for hunting, there wouldn't *be* any foxes – they'd all be shot or poisoned by the farmers.' Pufelli was plainly in no mood to accept this familiar argument: she showed her fangs and growled until the enemy moved away, and then wagged her tail in relief.

At Port Said I had the chance of varying the foxes' somewhat monotonous diet. There, in the ship's lounge, a magnificent conjuring show was staged by the famous gully-gully men; and it was astonishing to see how they could produce day-old chicks from a man's beard or a young lady's blouse or the middle of a pack of cards. The show was excellent, but the chicks were in a bad way; so I approached one of the men afterwards, and asked him to quote me a price for them. Presumably he thought that I wanted to eat them myself, and he assured me that there was no meat on them, none at all. He had a much better commodity on offer: 'You buy postcards?' he asked hopefully, ferreting in a leather bag and bringing out some extremely unladylike specimens. But eventually after some argument I convinced him that I did want the chicks, and we agreed on a price of 1s 6d for each stringy and breathless little bird.

In view of their supper that night my foxes may have come to think of Port Said as a gourmet's paradise.

Each day the orange glow of the dawn would appear slowly on the horizon of the Gulf of Aden, and soon afterwards the flying fish would appear, dancing tirelessly in the ship's wake The temperature rose rapidly and almost unendurably, until the top deck – cooled by the wind of the ship's movement – was the only comfortable place to be. So on we ploughed,

B*

through the gulf, round and down towards Mombasa, passing the arid coast of Somaliland, where the blinding whiteness of the sandy shore contrasted splendidly with the sapphire blue of the sea.

During these carefree days I had time to reflect on how I had spent the seven or so years since leaving school, and on the reason why I wanted to gather together a collection of animals during my forthcoming travels in Africa.

Two years in the Rhodesia and Nyasaland Staff Corps had convinced me that I was not cut out for a military career; but during this period I had travelled widely – in the Congo, in Northern and Southern Rhodesia, in Nyasaland, and in the Union of South Africa. In those countries I came to love the African continent, with its countless and fascinating species of mammals and birds; and I started to worry about the dangers which threatened many of these species as 'civilisation' intruded upon their ancient territories.

On my return to my home in Jersey I had been rather bewildered by the number of careers open to me and it was difficult to make a sensible choice between the various options. A family wine and spirit business, the Hong Kong Police, and tea planting in Assam would have all given me financial security, but there was something undefinably wrong with all of them. Considering this question seriously, examining the depths of my own mind and heart, I soon found out what was the matter: none of those admirable careers offered any scope for what I really wanted to do, for the greatest satisfaction that I had so far discovered in life. Somehow, on whatever terms, I needed to be working with animals. They could be wild or they could be domesticated; but in one way or another there had to be animals at the centre of my life.

So my destiny had crystallised. For me, those two years in Africa had been like a party which you attend in vague sociability, and there find yourself gazing into a new pair of eyes, and realise afterwards that life is never going to be the same again. But always, after some first moment of vision and vocation, one finds oneself brought down to earth with a bump. In the British Isles, I decided, livestock farming represented the obvious way of being involved with animals, and, although I found this interesting, and seventy-six cows kept me actively engaged for eight healthy months, I decided that it was not quite what I was looking for.

A three-month course in kennel management in the heart of Surrey was much more to my liking, and when the course came to an end, I felt that my vocation was now clear. I would return to Jersey and establish my own kennels there: I would breed dogs of every kind for the connoisseur, while keeping some of them to be my lifelong friends. My search for a suitable property was handicapped by the failure to get the necessary planning permission to build. Frustrated, I decided to take a temporary job until I could get this matter sorted out.

As often in people's lives, a casually taken temporary job turned out to be a major and decisive turning point in my life. I signed on for nothing more than brief summer employment at the newly created Jersey Zoological Park, the embryo of what later became Gerald Durrell's Jersey Wildlife Preservation Trust. I knew nothing about wild animals or the life of the zoo keeper, but I thought that in this environment I could become more widely acquainted with the animal kingdom, and especially with the possibilities of genuine relationships between man and beast.

I was soon to come under the spell of Gerald Durrell, and became totally captivated with the whole idea of breeding and the study of animals in captivity. I therefore put aside my ambition to work with dogs, and served for some two and a half years on the zoo staff; first working with tropical birds, and then with mammals.

Throughout the whole of this time my knowledge of the animal kingdom developed rapidly, and I accumulated a fairsized library, over which I spent many hours of my free time. There was so much to learn, and I began to regret the time that I had wasted in Africa. There I had been, in one of the world's great reservoirs of wildlife, and I had missed practically all my opportunities for learning about it.

Gradually, but on an increasing scale, thoughts of this kind began to haunt my mind. Anybody who has been there will tell you that Africa has a way of getting into the bloodstream and obsessing the mind; now it started to pull me. Fortunately these sentiments coincided with a small legacy, not a fortune, but enough to finance an animal-collecting expedition of my own. I had a lot of friends in southern Africa who could be counted upon to help me in such an enterprise. I was single, twenty-four years old, without ties. What was to hold me back? Thanks to the long-sighted kindness of Gerald Durrell, I was given every encouragement, as well as leave of absence, with the assurance that when I returned, my job would still be available if I wanted it.

At Mombasa I left the ship as I wanted to see something of the East African game reserves before going south to start my animal collection. The foxes were supposed to stay on board until Durban; but they were both feeling the heat rather badly, so I took them ashore with me and sent them off to Pretoria by air.

Soon I was installed in The Moorings, a small hotel in Mombasa. It had been raining almost continuously for three weeks, and the air was full of the intoxicating warm earthy smell of the African wet season. Parts of Kenya, in fact, were in a state of emergency: the rains had caused the River Tana to overflow, isolating a number of tribes, destroying crops extensively, and cutting communications by road and rail.

But none of this came home to me as I sat at breakfast enjoying my first contacts with the birds and animals of Africa, thinking already of capture. There were African pied crows, a dazzle of black and white as they quarrelled over worms and the crusts and crumbs of my breakfast; there were countless lizards, utterly motionless and then flicking across the polished floor of the verandah when the hotel's terrier came after them. On my second evening a cream-faced African hedgehog climbed into my bedroom and on to my mosquito net, digging its quills in as though it sought my intimate company. I soon felt that a month in this hotel would bring me all I wanted, and might even pay for my trip; but I had larger plans than that.

I walked under the palm trees, the red soil dyeing my shoes; I passed bare-footed Africans, smiling in the warm torrents of rain; frogs were chorusing from the overflowing storm gutters: I felt a love of Africa, a feeling that I belonged there. The colour and history of the place were all about me. There was Fort Jesus, built by the Portuguese and the scene of many bloody battles in the past, later used as a prison by the British, now a museum; ancient cannons were still mounted as though to command the old harbour; picturesque dhows brought in their cargoes of dates, raw salt, spices; the streets were crowded and jostling with Indians, Africans, Europeans; and the Mombasa Club still stood there, a monument to colonialism, with its polished floors, its silently moving servants, and its fine array of English sporting periodicals all set out on a long polished table beneath a revolving fan. Many worlds met here.

But I had to move on, and I took a night train to Nairobi. There I met the sad news that the Nairobi National Park was closed because of the floods. This was a blow. It had been my main intention to collect animals in what was then called Southern Rhodesia; but before that I had hoped to see the major national parks in East Africa, proceeding south from Nairobi, in the first instance, by the road to Arusha. This road was now closed; so I decided to wait until conditions improved, and in the meantime, to accept the kindly offered hospitality of a coffee farmer who lived at Ruiru, near Nairobi.

Even here conditions were damp and difficult. A nearby river was in spate, and its muddy waters rampaged through the vegetation: weaver birds found their beautifully woven nests destroyed and their eggs lost, and they flew about in agitation and grief.

Wandering near this farm I saw a tubular roll of bark suspended from the lower branches of a blue gum tree; and in my curiosity I prodded it with a stick. This rash action was rewarded at once by the emergence of several very angry squadrons of wild bees, which zoomed after me at full power in the best traditions of Fighter Command. I managed to get away; and later I discovered that tubular beehives of this kind were a speciality that originated with the Wakambo tribe. Seasoned bark would be rolled up, rather like a brandy snap, packed with leaves of a kind that the bees found alluring, and then hung up from some tree to attract useful tenants: I would have been more careful if I had known about this, and about the fact that while these wild bees always hate to be disturbed, they are particularly touchy during the rainy season. This was not the only occasion on which I picked on the hardest way of learning some fairly simple lesson.

Here I was, then, on a large spacious farm: a farmhouse, and a thousand acres of planted coffee around it. Even so, there was an atmosphere of siege, a hangover from Mau Mau days: the windows were barred like those of a top-security jail, there was a locked armoury built into a wall, the dogs were trained to let no African on to the premises apart from the permanent house staff, and even they had to be outside when the nightly ritual of locking and checking took place. But during the day things were easier: I saw the coffee beans drying in the sun, spread out along strips of matting, line after line of them, while groups of Africans worked industriously and contentedly, grading and packing the beans. So far this area had not been affected by the activities of the land-freedom army.

I brooded over the troubles that men make for one another, and for the animal world as well. Nature may be red in tooth and claw, but at least she is innocent of racial, religious, and political hatreds: the wild animals of Africa have no worries apart from the task of feeding themselves in the coolness of the early morning and then again in the evening, with the heat of the day spent in shady relaxation. In Nairobi I visited an exhibition that had been promoted by the East African Wildlife Society: they had taken over a big shop window and were displaying a collection of animal snares that had been confiscated from Africans and were forbidden by the very humane game laws. The idea was to educate people – to make them see how cruel and barbaric these snares were. But it worked out rather differently. A great many Africans came to see the exhibition, some of them from remote places; but it was found that they were returning to their villages and compounds with drawings of the various snares on display, being very glad of this chance to improve their own snaring techniques. The exhibition was hastily closed.

I spent a fortnight at the coffee farm; and then, since the road to Arusha in the south was still inaccessible because of the continuing torrential rains, I decided to change my plans. Kisumu, to the north-west of Nairobi, is on the shore of Lake Victoria: if I went there by train, I should be able to continue southwards by water. From Kisumu the MV *Victoria* took me around the north of the lake and then southwards on the Ugandan side to Mwanza (Tanzania): it was here, just over a hundred years previously – in the early morning of 3 August, 1858 – that John Henning Speke became the first white man to set eyes on the immense stretch of inland water, later naming it after his sovereign.

To get to Southern Rhodesia (Rhodesia) I travelled by train, bus and lorry by way of Tabora, Itigi and Mbeya, then over the border into Northern Rhodesia (Zambia) and by way of Ndola to Lusaka. I had been there before, during the emergency of 1956, when I was attached to the Northern Rhodesia Regiment. So I revisited the barracks opposite Government House, and after having renewed my acquaintance with the regiment's mascots, two Kavirondo crane, I went to see the adjutant in the hope that he had some type of vehicle travelling south to Salisbury. My luck was in, a seven-ton Army Bedford was leaving that very evening, and as an ex-regular myself, I was given permission to travel in it.

A light easterly breeze cooled the cab of the Bedford as we descended to the one-span suspension bridge at Chirundu which spans the Zambezi between Northern and Southern Rhodesia – now, between Zambia and Rhodesia. Frogs piped us on board the bridge: nightjars flew up in our faces as though from underground. The world-famous mosquitoes at Chirundu could not get at us while the truck still moved. But they got their chance when we stopped on the bridge beneath its great structure to gaze upon the river and the light bush of the escarpment: I have seldom been so extensively eaten.

Then, with the two NCOs, we motored on southwards through the night, while I learnt a first-hand account of the sad story of the Central African Federation, and the rather gloomy prospects for the people of those lands, white and black alike. I was dropped in the heart of Salisbury at Old Meikles Hotel, where I shaved, breakfasted, and feeling suitably invigorated I hired a vehicle to take me out to the Mazoe/Glendale area of Southern Rhodesia where I had been invited to set up my base.

CHAPTER 2

The First Quarry

DOUET Farm sprawled across the top of a small kopje: a long building roofed with thatch of varying antiquity, with a brick chimney at each end, tilting and precarious.

I was greeted by Major Robin Falla, my host, a tall hefty man with deep-set eyes and a jovial sort of face. As he strode around, his broad shoulders aggressively braced, he put me in mind of a gorilla: at any moment (it seemed) he might start to beat his chest in a fine display of threat and challenge. In point of fact Robin was much more likely to offer you his kingdom than to exclude you from it. He was an old soldier, an officer successively in three different armies – the Jersey Militia, the British Army and the Indian Army. With this last career cut short by Indian independence, he came with his family to settle here in Rhodesia and to wage war upon the bush. Already this campaign was succeeding, a profitable tobacco and dairy farm emerging from the raw countryside.

Immediately, before I was even allowed to enter the house, Robin led me to see his three large tobacco barns, home built with home-baked bricks. They were tall buildings, faintly ecclesiastical, cathedral like: in two of them I saw a maze of horizontal blue gum poles above my head, with tobacco leaves draped over them, extending upwards like a thatch as far as I could see. Heat rose from flues below – ultimately, from a coal furnace outside – and caressed these leaves until they attained the pallid jaundice-like yellow colour that showed them to be fully cured.

All this was interesting enough; but for me, the third barn was the important one. Here the flues had been removed: the place was empty, and Robin was offering it to me as temporary accommodation for whatever animals I might catch. He only stipulated that any lions brought in should be kept away from his cattle.

This was great kindness on his part and a most practical suggestion. The height of the building was not really essential for my purpose, but its spaciousness was exactly what I needed. At once I started to divide it up mentally into runs and cages, daydreaming of wonderful success, of countless extraordinary animals filling this place and needing eventually to be transferred into travelling cages, and then shipped home, and then... My mind went racing ahead, but I pulled it up sharply, reminding myself that I had no experience and no certainty at all of catching anything. The whole expedition might still be a failure, with no animal smells coming to challenge the tobacco smells of this splendid barn.

Then we went to the farmhouse, and I was introduced to the family, to Robin's wife Pris, and their two children Roselle and James. There was the nicest kind of welcome, and then we all sat outside on the *stoep* or verandah, enjoying the fresh air and the evening breeze, protected by screens from the countless insects which were attracted by the light but had to whine frustratedly outside.

Whisky was brought, and they drank a toast to the magnificent collection that I was to assemble. Just then a kitten ran out from under the sofa, leapt into the air, pounced upon a disembowelled slipper that was lying beside me, and started to savage it murderously. Ordinary kittenish behaviour, you might think; but this was no ordinary kitten, it was a young serval which they had found on the farm a month or so earlier, orphaned and alone. Soon she dropped the slipper to consider me: her long ears flicked with curiosity, and she watched every movement I made, narrowly and suspiciously. I held out my hand invitingly, but she ignored it and returned to finish off the slipper: a lovely creature, her yellow-golden coat marked with irregular brown to black spots, her short tail swishing.

'Well, and what's going to be your first victim?' asked Robin, in the smart regimental manner of a senior officer at an order-group. Dismayed, cornered, I gulped at my whisky. What could I say? I cudgelled my brain. Should I confess that ... well, that I'd been wholly absorbed by the business of travel during these last few weeks, and that my *precise* itinerary and plan were – well, a shade imperfect in detail, and that perhaps ... ? I could hardly answer truthfully, and say that I intended to catch anything that came along and proved catchable: the build up had been too colourful for that, I was typed already as the intrepid hunter with some masterful plan of conquest. There was a danger of anticlimax and disillusionment.

Possibly Robin thought that I was hesitating because my plans were too grand and complex to be explained easily. Or possibly not. At any rate, he came to my rescue with a list of suggestions: 'Serval cat, caracal, jackal, hunting dogs, civets, genets, mongoose, porcupines, wild pig – there's lots of that kind of stuff around the farm, you could pick them up pretty easily.' He spoke apologetically, as though I had bigger stuff in mind and would hardly be bothered by these rats and mice and such small deer. But I cheered up: if these animals were so easy to find, I was not going to be embarrassed by an empty tobacco barn.

Our glasses were refuelled and clinked together. The serval kitten, tired of that slipper, decided to attack my feet instead: first she tore at my laces, then she lay back and fought my socks, kicking and scratching furiously. It was agony: I forced myself to remember that I was a great lover of animals, and used the whisky as an anaesthetic.

The evening proceeded. At sundown Roselle and James were put to bed: three hours later Pris followed them; but Robin and I stayed up, with the drinks that were nominally 'sun-downers' continuing to flow. My arrival, Robin explained, made this a special occasion: I was to find that every evening at Douet Farm was, on one pretext or another, a special occa-

sion. Eventually, by way of a climax to the evening, Robin
stood up formally by the fire in his shorts and shirt and told
an African house boy to bring in the farm's mascot. I cringed
in instinctive terror: my head was swimming, and my legs
and feet were suffering horribly from the serval kitten's attentions. What kind of animal would be inflicted upon me now?
I looked around for an escape route; but at that moment the
door crashed open, and 170 lb of African bush pig rocketed
into the room. This was Porky, a formidable mascot indeed:
bulky, covered with coarse wiry red-brown bristles, white
bristled on his face, his ears tufted. He stood downwind of me;
backed a little, as though to break cover before charging; and
then trotted forward in all gentleness to sniff my hand, his
eyes bright and friendly, his grin and grunt most charming.

I breathed again.

So Robin and I drank some more toasts, naming countless
animals that must be included in the collection; and then he
took his lamp – there was no electricity – and led me down a
whitewashed corridor to bed. We left Porky snoring under
the table in a rather pig-like manner, but the serval kitten
followed me, fighting my shoe-laces to the last. I felt that I
was taking part in some dream or pantomime of Africa: my
host bade me goodnight, the lamp went out with a hiss that
terrified the serval out of her wits, and I collapsed into a
series of dreams, each one ending with the escape of some
animal from my keen pursuit.

The morning came, and with it the secretary of the local
farming club. There were two ideas in his mind. For one thing,
some porcupines had been making a mess of his front lawn;
and since there was a well-known professional hunter staying
in the district, perhaps I wouldn't mind catching them? Then,
would I give a talk to the monthly meeting of the local farmers
at the country club? I accepted the first of these invitations at
once: it sounded as if it might be good sport to dig out crested
porcupines and net them – or try to net them – when they
made a run for it. But to lecture a crowd of Rhodesian
farmers … this was quite a different matter. I had only spoken

1 KEAN, B. H.

M.D.: ONE DOCTOR'S ADVENTURES AMONG THE FAMOUS

04 027547

051990

in public once, as best man at my brother's wedding: once was enough, and in any case I could hardly speak with authority on the catching of wild animals when I had never caught one in my life. I drew breath to explain this, when Robin interposed to say that this was an *excellent* idea, and that he would have some members round for drinks afterwards. The matter was out of my hands, it seemed.

The farmers' secretary said that he'd come back after lunch and take me to where these porcupines had dug themselves in, so that I could mount my assault upon them. Meanwhile, Robin and I took the Land-Rover and went off to the compound in search of an African who could be my assistant.

It was an unpromising search. The track swung sharply round a clump of blue gum trees, and there in front of us was a scattering of small mud hovels. African women leant against their doorposts with folded arms: listless children tumbled everywhere among the dogs and hens that scratched and scuffled in the dust. The boss boy, Moses by name, raised a mud-encrusted bush hat, spat violently, bellowed out to his fellows, and assembled a group of them for my approval and choice.

I knew what sort of man I wanted, and by no stretch of the imagination could any of these be regarded as filling the bill. I asked Robin whether there were any alternative prospects, but he wasn't hopeful: it was almost impossible to get reliable labour without patiently sifting through an enormous number of candidates. So, on his advice, I settled for John Carpenter, from Mozambique and mission educated, whose self-chosen surname indicated his qualifications and skill. He would, he said, be able to make all the cages I needed. (In my experience, such claims need to be taken with a big pinch of salt. Cut them down by fifty per cent, and you get something like the real picture.)

With that problem solved for the time being at least, I continued my conducted tour of Robin's farm. Its border on the west was a small tributary of the Mazoe River, and we drove by this stream, its red muddy waters running deep in this sixth week of the rainy season. A hammerheaded stork – locally called a hammerkop – was standing in the shallows: disturbed by the noise of the car, it flew up into its big ramshackle nest of twigs. On we drove, needing to use four-wheel drive on some of the lower tracks: I was shown the pump house, from which large galvanised tanks of water were taken daily to the farm buildings by tractor and trailer, and eventually we came back to the house.

We had seldom been out of sight of it: together with the tobacco barns, it stood on the highest point for some distance around, commanding wide views not only of the farm but of the uncultivated bush around it. Because of this strong position, it had been chosen by the local security forces to be a rallying point for all the women and children of the neighbourhood in the event of any dangerous emergency. I was shown two ten-foot numbers made up of bricks that had been sunk into the earth and whitewashed: it was their function to make the ·farm easily identifiable from the air. Under heavy penalties each farmer had the legal duty of marking his farm with such numbers, and of keeping them weeded and whitewashed for easy visibility.

After lunch I felt a sense of occasion. A big moment was coming. So far it had all been travel and preparation: now I was to start the actual job, the actual collecting of real animals.

I left Douet Farm with the farmers' secretary and also with John Carpenter: we had four nets, two spades, and a pickaxe. The car twisted and bumped along the strip roads, the country dotted with rocks and little clumps of vegetation in between the rich tobacco lands of the European farmers.

I felt a shade nervous. Nobody can say that I wasn't well educated: even so, I had never qualified in porcupine catching. The nearest thing in England would be the badger, which lives in a very similar sort of earth: but the nature walks of my schooldays had not led up to even an ordinary level certificate in badger trapping. I would have to rely upon whatever hunting instincts I had inherited from my prehistoric ancestors.

I was shown the big hole that was (presumably) the porcupines' front door : it was guarded by a cloud of midges. In this kind of situation the great thing is to appear to know what you're doing. So I rapped out a business-like command, and told John to fetch me a long flexible stick, which he immediately did, at the cost of heavy damage to some cultivated shrubs nearby; and then I flung myself down and prodded far into the dark dirty hole.

Vaguely in my mind was a notion that every such earth had two holes, a front door and a back door. The task was easy : you just had to light a fire at one hole and wait with your nets at the other. The trouble was that there *was* no second hole. So I improvised a different plan, thereby displaying the initiative and attack that has always marked the British officer in his country's hour of need : we would dig a series of shafts down into successive stretches of the tunnel, using my long stick as a kind of range-finder or target indicator. Spades were fetched, and two of the 'boys' from this farm got cheerfully to work. I had staked my nets over the hole : the midges flew through it freely, but a porcupine (I calculated) would not.

I seemed to have underestimated the whole business. It took nearly an hour of sweating and grunting before this first shaft was completed : it had to be a big shaft if I was to reach down into it with my sapling and feel out the direction of the tunnel's next stretch, and there were a lot of tough tangled roots to be dug through. And so far, we had only moved eight feet along the winding tunnel, or a mere five feet as measured directly.

Somewhat daunted, I marked the spot for the second shaft and netted the first. The pickaxe was now brought into action to help the spades, and the steady pounding of metal into hard earth was accompanied by the increasingly loud grunts of the African diggers, as they drew breath after every stroke. To them it was an entirely pointless exercise.

The second shaft was only a little deeper than the first, but it took nearly twice as long to dig. Like a good officer I was ready to share in the men's hardships, so I took my turn at the digging : this showed that I had the right attitude but it wasn't impressive otherwise. However, we were making progress : at any rate the tunnel was getting narrower and the midges were getting more and more interested, which presumably meant something. The light was fading, however: should we finish three shafts and then call it a day? My farmer friend thought not: he would bring lanterns if it got too dark.

I felt uncertain. Were there really porcupines down this tunnel? There was certainly a pungent smell of dung and decay: if nothing was living there now, something had been living there recently. So I rallied my troops to further exertions, in spite of their increasing gloom. The smell got worse, and my hopes revived. Suddenly, when the third shaft was nearly finished, we heard a loud furious hissing sound, as though compressed air or steam was escaping through a leaky valve. Everybody turned enquiringly to the expert: unfortunately I had never heard the noise made by a porcupine, but I felt sure that it wasn't like this. So the two Africans climbed out of the shaft and I climbed in: the bottom gave way at once, and my feet plunged into the tunnel, narrowly missing something that clawed and spat at me savagely and then dashed along the tunnel, past the second shaft and the first, to end up tangled and fighting in the net that we had staked over the original hole.

It was a small African wild cat, a creature not unlike the wild cat of Scotland, with tabby markings on a light orange-yellow coat and black rings round the legs and the rather short tail. There was total fury upon its black-striped face: if it had been able to wriggle past the net! But there it was, tangled and trapped. I wrapped another net round it for extra safety, and told the boys that they would get a good *bonseller* for the day's work. As a campaign against porcupines it had failed, but I was satisfied with the result.

I carried my bundle carefully into the farmhouse to show it to the farmer secretary, sending for the one crate that I had at the ready. I shut the doors and windows carefully to prevent any escape bid, and then, alone with John, I cautiously began work on the struggling bundle. John backed nervously against the door: the cat was twisting and striking in all directions at

(*above*) An armful of orangs; (*right*) Clio, my Chacma Baboon.

With N'Pongo, a lowland gorilla: (*above*) 'I believe there is some pâté de maison inside this.' (*centre*) 'Well, give me some!'; (*below*) '*That* was worth while!'

once; it was in a mood for real trouble, and I felt nervous myself. But I managed to keep the initiative, manipulating the net so that the brute never quite got its balance: I bellowed to John to face the music, and together we managed to get it crated without bloodshed.

The farmer came in to see what we'd achieved, and rashly put his face rather close to the wire mesh which provided ventilation for the crate: he must have been surprised to find himself very nearly being mauled by a wild cat where he had expected to see a porcupine. I started to apologise for my failure, but he insisted on congratulating me: he had lost a lot of poultry recently, and I had caught the killer. So I felt free to join in the general excitement. John was anxious to go off and tell the other 'boys' about his courageous single-handed achievement; I gave him some beer money to share around, and told him to be back in half an hour.

An hour later there was still no sign of him, and the farmer and I started back to Douet without him. 'What was the first animal you ever caught?' I was asked as we drove along. I could hardly explain that it was the very animal that was now with us in the car: so I laughed the question off with the suggestion of a juvenile mousetrap, and was glad to find that the farmer wasn't going to take the matter further. It's never kind to disillusion people.

The next morning, just after sunrise, I sauntered down to the tobacco barns at Douet to have another look at the founder member of my collection. There by the barns sat John, looking extremely sheepish and red about the eyes: he probably expected to get the sack. I took a firm line and explained that as he plainly couldn't carry his liquor, he wasn't to touch it – except on his days off – while he was in my employ. He had paid for his orgy with an exhaustingly long walk.

Twelve hours in the crate had not brought the cat to any state of resignation: it lunged at me through the wires. But when Robin appeared, with his loud booming voice, it crouched back in terror.

'Ah,' said Robin, 'you'll have to find it a mate. What sex is

C

this one?' I agreed that it was important to ascertain its sex and then to find a mate, though I couldn't see how either task could be done. So I deferred this problem diplomatically. This crate was too small to be used except for a very short time: I had better go into Salisbury with John to buy some materials to make proper travelling cages to house a general collection. This cat's love life could wait.

I had bought a Vanguard ¾-ton pick-up, and John and I went bouncing along the strip roads until we reached a proper tarmac surface on the outskirts of Salisbury. I bought a good deal of two-by-two timber, many sheets of plywood, some wire mesh, and packets of screws, hinges, nails, catches, and locks. Then I called in at the Salisbury Museum and met Mr Reay Smithers, who was the director of Rhodesian museums, and also his deputy, Dr Brain. Mr Smithers told me that he had a good collection of waterfowl at his home, which I was welcome to inspect before I left the country; Dr Brain had a collection of live vervet monkeys and was studying them. Altogether they were most helpful: they even offered me a pair of black-backed jackals, on condition that I removed them at once.

Things were certainly moving: it was only the second day of my task, and already I had two jackals and a wild cat. I began to believe in my assumed character of an expert trapper.

So John and I loaded the pick-up with all the materials and the crated jackals. To judge by the noise they made they didn't recognise salvation when it came: they had been brought in by a farmer for the museum, and if I hadn't come at that precise moment they would very soon have been stuffed.

I drove back to Douet with a powerful feeling of success, half expecting various wild animals to leap aboard the pick-up and demand to be caged. On the way, just as we were approaching a small African settlement of mushroom shaped huts, a hen came charging across the road and collided heavily with the Vanguard. The impact proving fatal, we were immediately surrounded by a crowd of aggrieved Africans, loud in their claim for compensation. There were the makings of an ugly scene; so I leant back and slapped the sides of the jackals' box, from which a fearsome noise came at once. The villagers backed away nervously, expecting a pack of mad dogs to be set upon them: even John, safe in the cab, wound up the window. Having thus re-established my mastery over things, I pressed ten shillings into the hand of a wizened old lady by way of compensation for the deceased hen, and drove on.

Back at Douet Farm I made it my first task to get the jackals out of their crate and into a spacious run. So we got to work in the tobacco barn, and managed to wire off one corner with six-foot wire, fixing the top of this to the lowest of the blue gum poles that were meant to carry drying tobacco. Then, after unloading our timber and other materials into the barn, we brought the crate across and introduced the jackals to their new home. They seemed to prefer the security of the crate, which was hardly surprising, since my wild cat expressed her dislike of them in a very threatening way.

Robin was deeply impressed with what I'd achieved. 'Dammit, man, just a couple of days, and you've got half the animal kingdom already!' We sat long over our drinks, and he told me many stories of his tiger-shooting adventures and escapades in India – small stuff, as he confessed, when compared to my own heroic work.

The early morning is the best time for hunting and trapping, and I decided that I would have to cut down on these over-lubricated late nights, deeply enjoyable though they were. So I turned to the deployment of the traps that I had brought from England, and for the next few days I made a point of rising early to see what treasure they held for me.

They were big wire traps, tunnel shaped, with a hook in the middle from which some appetising bait could be suspended. Beneath this hook was a treacherous platform, which, when trodden upon, would release a spring mechanism so that doors were instantly clicked and locked shut at each end of the tunnel. I set these traps each night, varying the bait from eggs to raw meat to fruit to seeds: each morning I would approach them breathlessly on tiptoe, which was a bit pointless – if

I'd caught anything, no amount of noise would frighten it away. But I never had caught anything: there was the trap each time, untouched, the bait still there.

Robin came to my rescue. 'I don't want to teach my grandmother to suck eggs; but you could do what the Indians do – smear the traps with animal dung. Sorry, I'm being silly: you've probably got some good reason for wanting the traps to have a human smell.' 'Yes, of course I know about that technique,' I said hastily: 'but before doing that, I thought I might experiment a bit with – well, I shan't bother you with the details now, it's rather technical.' 'Sorry,' said Robin, 'you know best.'

The next time, therefore, I did that rather unpleasant smearing; the traps stank all right afterwards, and not of humankind. I also sprinkled their floors with earth, so as to conceal the difference between the trip-platforms and the rest; and I camouflaged the tops and sides. I did all this, including the arrangement of the bait, with gloved hands. Nobody could say I didn't know my job.

I set the traps now in a part of the farm where there were a good many boulders; and I noticed among them some very brightly coloured lizards, which basked peacefully in the sun until I came near, but then flashed away into crevices in these rocks. Presumably they hadn't met an animal trapper before, but they were taking no chances and always got away. I was intrigued by this challenge and by the lizards themselves, and after setting my traps, I went back to the farm to make a kind of butterfly-net which might defeat them.

I made a big one, and returned to my hunting ground in the afternoon with my mind wholly upon lizards. I had almost forgotten my traps until a sudden noise from one of them caught my attention. I ran up and saw a slender weasel-like animal inside, with a brown body and a long tail tipped with black: on seeing me it panicked, running up and down the trap in a frenzy. I picked the trap up carefully, making sure that my hands were safe from angry teeth, and walked the half mile back to the barn.

There I found John engaged in some low-speed carpentry: he grinned guiltily when he saw me. I put the trap down – the jackals were deeply interested in this strong-smelling new arrival – told John what kind of cage I wanted now, and went off to the farmhouse in search of *Mammals of Central Africa*, by Asterly Maberly. This useful book made it clear that my guest was a mongoose – the slender mongoose, to judge by its shape in the picture. I had never seen one before, so I took the book back to confirm this identification.

It took us two hours to complete a cage for the mongoose. John wanted to nail everything, which was easier, but I insisted on screws. He certainly looked the part of a carpenter, with a pencil behind his ear, a piece of paper with lines and numbers in one hand, a hammer or screwdriver in the other. But his actual performance was less impressive; and when the mongoose cage was finished, complete with its front of machine-made wire mesh, it was necessary to put plugs of wood into the gaps between the wire and the frame. Otherwise the animal could have simply walked out. But John was very pleased with himself: to sober him up I said that if the mongoose got away he would have to recapture it himself.

The cage was now ready, but the mongoose decided to stay in the trap. I coaxed, I pleaded, I tilted the trap: I even put a couple of eggs into the cage as an inducement. But he sat fast, glaring at me. This time my problem was solved for me by one of the jackals: it sprang at the wire of its enclosure, and the noise caused the mongoose to leap forward in panic and into the cage, where I had the door shut upon him in an instant.

Now there were four animals in the barn. I saw that I would soon need more cages, and I begged John to apply himself more seriously to the art of carpentry. I didn't want to have my collection escaping: I envisaged having a lot of them before long, varied and valuable. But now luck seemed to turn against me. However carefully I baited and camouflaged my traps, however richly aromatic the dung with which I anointed them, they remained obstinately empty. As for the lizards ... their agility, so pleasing to behold, proved to be a trapper's utter frustration. I would creep up upon them clutching my butterfly-net and admiring the red and blue and yellow and orange of their spots and stripes: they sat immobile on the scorching rock in their trendy gear, apparently asleep or unaware, and it looked too easy, but their radar was in perfect order, and they always flicked away at precisely the last microsecond. Soon I gave up, and returned to the animals I already had. Who *wants* lizards, anyway?

I would rise at 6.30 each morning and go down to see my collection. The jackals and the mongoose ate well and seemed to accept their destiny, but the wild cat refused to touch food or to accept my friendship, spitting with incurable hatred instead. In theory John helped me with the task of cleaning out the cages and watering and feeding the animals: in practice he seemed so frightened of all animals that I had to do nearly all the work, while he just passed plates and shovels and so forth to me from a very safe distance, grinning nervously. But by breakfast-time each day the job was done, leaving the rest of the day free for other activities.

For John there was the simple task of cage building. But as well as persevering with my traps, I had to look ahead: if I was to export animals from the Federation, there would be permits to get and arrangements to make. So I made a trip to Salisbury for those purposes; I had to see the Game Department, the Veterinary Department, and the people at the airline office. Everybody was very helpful, but the airline's freight manager was baffled by the vagueness of my plans. He wanted to know the exact weights and dimensions of every crate: but although I had been fairly successful so far, I had no means of estimating the scale on which I would eventually be flying my private menagerie out of the country. It might be huge, it might be very small. These details would have to wait.

Meanwhile, rumour seemed to be telling all Salisbury about my activities, and I found myself confronted by an anxious and quick-talking young reporter who – in the intervals of covering the tobacco auctions – wanted to know about myself and my background, and how I had first achieved the success which made me now a well-known professional trapper. Embarrassed once again, I changed the subject, and told him that I had once been a regular soldier in the Rhodesian and Nyasaland Staff Corps. He scented a story at once: EX-RHODESIAN SOLDIER TURNS BIG GAME HUNTER, 'BRING 'EM BACK ALIVE,' SAYS EX-RHODESIAN REGULAR, and such other headlines were plainly in his mind as his pencil flew. I tried to get him interested also in the study of wild animals, their care and breeding in captivity, the importance of conservation, and such subjects; but his mind was already back in the tobacco auction rooms, and he gulped down his beer, shook my hand, and was off at high speed.

On my way back to Glendale I called in upon Mike and Winky Smoelke, who were friends of Robin and Pris partly because they had similar pets. (Even in England, I have noticed that people often become specially friendly with those who have the same unusual breed of dog.) We had afternoon tea on the verandah while the three cats of the household chased around in a suitably crazy cat-like fashion. Two of them were serval cats, well domesticated by now, while the third can only be described in contradictory terms: it was a tame wild cat. All three, however, were tame only in respect of their owners: they would not allow anybody else to touch them, and I was careful not to try. But they were lovely to watch, with their agile leapings and their mad games; and I could easily imagine how they could kill small antelopes – duikers, for example – with those powerful legs and teeth. I studied the wild cat with particular interest, not having seen one in the adult state before: I hoped that my own kitten would exhaust its present ferocity and become as friendly as this one.

Then one of the farm boys brought in a 'legervarn' or rock monitor. Mike took this reptile out of a sack and handed it across the table to me, perhaps not with the actual intention of upsetting me: he held it behind the head, steadying its body with his other hand, while its pointed tail trailed into the strawberry jam. This must be the correct way of handling such brutes; so I gulped and grinned and swallowed and grabbed it, making brave noises of admiration. 'Well, if you like it so much, you can have it,' said Mike. I accepted gratefully, and dropped my first reptile into its sack with some relief.

The very appearance of a monitor would justify every observer in regarding these rapacious lizards, as the prototype of all dragons in fairy tales. It was a slender reptile with a strikingly long neck, elongated jaws, well developed legs with long sharp claws and a whip-like tail. Like all other monitors, it was covered with a very strong, rough skin, which the fangs of the smaller venomous snake cannot penetrate. I soon found out nearly to my cost, that when it became excited it would inflate itself, give a warning salvo of hisses, then open its mouth and attempt to strike the intruder with powerful and well aimed blows of its tail. When picked up during further encounters, it would attempt to bite, and scratch, particularly with the claws on the back legs which lashed out with its tail.

That evening I borrowed one of Robin's horses for a ride over the farmlands. But it was six years or so since I had ridden, and I was horribly out of practice: my knee-grip had gone, I could only rise in the saddle very uncertainly, and the expected gallop became a walk. Slowly, therefore, I rode down the winding muddy track to the banks of the Mazoe. There, between the rows of tobacco, I saw four long-legged bustards: they strolled about and nodded to each other, like four elderly clergymen at a theological conference. Perhaps because I was mounted they seemed to have no fear of me.

The sun was just beginning to set. Two brace of helmeted guinea-fowl took to flight, protesting noisily at being disturbed; warned by them, a ram reedbuck sped past on my left. The sun sank deeper, an orange glow like barley sugar spreading over the farmlands: a pair of grey touracos uttered their call from across the river, a nasal 'go away, go away', while a tropical yellow bishop bird flew up into the towering blue gum trees by the river side, looking much refreshed by its evening bathe.

And so, in the peace of the evening, I turned back towards the farm. My mount scented home, however, and his walk accelerated into an uncontrolled canter, tending towards a gallop when I tried to pull him up with the snaffle. So I abandoned myself to fate and concentrated on the single problem of staying aboard: we sped in steeplechase fashion, and most dangerously, among the ant-hills and potholes, and we made it. For him, the stable; for me, drinks and dinner in good company.

CHAPTER 3

Monkeys and Tranquillisers

BEFORE long I was able to feel that my base at Douet Farm was soundly and agreeably established. John had managed to make some cages in the tobacco barn, and some travelling-boxes too; he had even mastered the art of feeding the animals and cleaning out their cages without damage to himself, and was very proud of this new skill. I had made a somewhat random start to my collection, and I felt that the time was now ripe for me to go away and do some planned trapping of specifically chosen animals. Later on the larger collection would need my continual presence; but for the time being I could leave it in John's hands, with Robin and Pris keeping a supervisory eye upon him.

Tucked away in the Vumba Mountain-Mellsetter area, in the south-eastern part of Southern Rhodesia, lived a sub-species of the white-throated guenon, otherwise known as the Stair's or Mozambique monkey, or (among zoologists) as *Cercopithecus albogularis erythrarchus*. This kind of monkey was very seldom seen in captivity; if I managed to catch four or five of them I would have the nucleus of a breeding group, which the Jersey Zoo would be very pleased to have.

So I loaded up the truck with five travelling-boxes, two wire traps, and my nets, together with my personal effects – excluding, however, my grandmother's tin of disinfectant, which I left behind at Douet. And so I set forth. Since the rear suspension of the pick-up lacked the refinement of shock-absorbers,

I had a somewhat rough ride, bumping down the 280 miles to Umtali grimly rather than enjoyably, and with frequent halts: every so often the radiator would boil, sending clouds of steam up through the floor to cloud the windscreen. I then waited until things cooled off: the disease seemed incurable.

Reay Smithers had advised me to call at the small museum at Umtali, since he knew that they had the odd Stair's monkey in their live collection behind the building. The curator – a Captain Boathby – was only too glad to let me see this animal, also some vervet monkeys and a spotted hyena that was supposed to be tame.

The Stair's monkey and I looked into each other's eyes almost like a pair of lovers. She had interesting markings: the dorsal pelage was a speckled light grey with a tendency to olive green, her legs pale grey, her forearms and hands and feet black, her bright eyes ringed with light brown, her ears well camouflaged by yellowish-white tufts. In sharp contrast with the rest of her colouring, and especially with her black tail, she had a collar and underparts of dazzling white.

I was distracted from the study of this monkey beauty by Captain Boathby, who wanted to show me just how tame his hyena was. He called an African, who at once put on a heavy army greatcoat and – with no show of reluctance – unlatched the animal's cage and went in.

The spotted hyena had been asleep in a patch of sun; now he got up, looked narrowly at the intruder, and charged.

'He's a great one for a game!' said the Captain, admiringly. It looked to me like the kind of game that the Romans watched in their amphitheatres, the lions sporting playfully with the Christians. The hyena had got his teeth into the sleeve, held on like a wolf, and was leaping and pulling with furious malevolence. It went on and on, with the African grimacing with terror: I very much hoped that this was put on as a stage-effect for my benefit, but soon he looked genuinely punch drunk and in danger of being really hurt. At this point the Captain intervened, broke off the engagement, thanked the African, and told me proudly that to the best of his knowledge this was the only tame hyena in Africa. It wasn't quite my idea of tameness.

I now made him an offer for the Stair's monkey, but this was turned down since it had been at the museum for two years and had become quite a pet. The Captain thought that I would have no trouble in securing what I wanted in the Vumba Mountains. 'You can shoot a mother and then catch the young ones,' he said, 'or if you don't want to do that, you can always net your specimens by hiding tranquillisers in fruit. They get drowsy, and you can catch them before they get away.'

He gave me an introduction to a vet in Umtali, who – after questioning me carefully – wrote me out a prescription for some nembutal capsules. Suspicions of suicide were plainly in the chemist's mind when I came in and asked for an enormous quantity of sleeping pills. But when I told him my purpose, and stressed the cruelty of the only alternative method, he gave me what I wanted and wished me luck. The dose needed to be kept in proportion to the body weight of the animal, which was 30 to 38lbs in the case of an adult Stair's monkey: I would have to spead my drugged bananas over quite an area, to reduce the risk of a single monkey getting a big overdose and thus leaving this cruel world in the Hollywood fashion.

And so I left Umtali, down colourful avenues lined with flamboyant and mimosa trees, down plain tarmac roads which soon became dirt roads, and so on up into the Vumba Mountains. As I climbed, a thick mist or *guti* came rolling down from above, reducing visibility to ten yards or so: thick vegetation flanked the road, sometimes closing in overhead to form a tunnel, and then parting suddenly to reveal precipitous valleys, falling away on one side of the road or even on both sides. Thus, with the mist and the winding road and the danger of a fall, I had to proceed in bottom gear: this meant that, despite the cool moist air, the engine overheated even more often than usual.

I was heading for the famous Leopard's Rock Hotel, which had been built by Italian prisoners of war during the last war;

but, being very much preoccupied with the dangers of the drive, I missed two turnings and found myself at the end of a cul-de-sac. There was a house there: I left the engine to cool off once again, and went to ask for directions to the hotel. There I met a Lt-Col H. G. Sewerd, who drew a map for me and pressed a drink into my hand.

'Stair's monkeys!' he exclaimed. 'Damned things. They come down here from up by the summit, and they go through my orchards stealing everything. I shoot them when I can. But they're getting wise to me, much harder to bag.'

So I asked him about my chances of catching some of them alive. 'Nothing easier,' he said. 'Just shoot a mother and pick the youngster off her back. That's the only way.'

No, I explained; I never shot anything. That would be contrary to the philosophy of my whole expedition.

The Colonel raised his eyebrows, and to show what I was missing by reason of this eccentricity he brought out the skins of two specimens that he had shot. He had meant them to be used as rugs or spread over chairs; but the skins had not been cured properly and let off a pungent smell; his wife therefore insisted on relegating them to the attic.

Before I left England Dr Osman Hill had told me that he would be very glad to have any material relevant to the primates of Africa: he was writing an immense monograph, and needed more data for his sixth volume. I mentioned this to the Sewerds, and thus triggered off a domestic disagreement. To Mrs Sewerd this was a fine pretext for getting those smelly skins out of the house; but to the Colonel they were his own trophies, shot and mounted (however imperfectly) by himself, and he didn't want to part with them. The battle raged to and fro, ending with a compromise: I took one skin, and the Colonel kept the other. So I took my leave before he could change his mind, and made my way on to the Leopard's Rock Hotel.

It was almost empty: this was not the tourist season for the Vumba Mountains. The building was turreted, and stood out against a mountainside that was swathed in mist: I might have been visiting a castle in Argyllshire. I ate alone in a vast dining room, feeling very self-conscious because of the numerous staff of liveried Africans, who stood there in shy silence, observing every mouthful that I took. I was glad to reach the solitude of my spacious bedroom.

I rose at 6.15 next morning, put a groundsheet cape around my shoulders, left the hotel by a back door, and set off through the thick vegetation on the mountainside. Some African pied crows squawked their astonishment at seeing me emerge from their private thickets: one of them followed me in deep curiosity, while a number of small red squirrels – later identified as the Swynnerton's red squirrel – dashed nervously around in the upper branches of the trees, their tails flickering.

I climbed higher. By the time the mists began to clear my feet and legs were saturated from the wet vegetation. Below me I could just see the tops of the hotel turrets, and, on the other side of the valley, the sun-drenched peaks of the mountains emerged from a sea of mist. Some black-faced vervet monkeys passed me to the left, leaping from one flexible branch to another, shaking the leaves and scattering showers as they went: some of them scampered down the heavy limbs of a baobab tree, crashed through the thin twigs in a manner that looked suicidal, caught their handhold further down, and continued along at unbroken pace. Birds were everywhere, pure-voiced choristers, singing their matins of gratitude for the light of daybreak.

The point was that this mountainside – according to the hotel manager – ought to have been thickly populated with Stair's monkeys. But I was unlucky: I stared every way with my powerful binoculars and found none. After an hour of searching I slithered down to the hotel, fortified myself with a good breakfast – invigilated, as before, by many shy attentive waiters – and ordered a packed lunch. I told the manager about my disappointment, and he lent me two of his men to show me the way to Castle Beacon. There, he explained, the Stair's monkey was *sure* to be seen.

So I drove as far as I could with these two Africans, and

with my traps and nets and my packet of tranquillisers: then we left the pick-up, shared the burdens around, and walked in single file towards the beacon. Above this, a long strip of forest had been cleared for the erection of telephone wires between the mountains and Umtali, and to serve also as a fire-break: this meant that if any monkey came down the mountainside, he would have to come down from the trees and make a dash through the grass, on the surface, before regaining the forest cover further below. I examined the grass and soon found their crossing place, with the grass trampled here and tunnelled there.

So I found an ant-hill, and used its soft soil to wipe my traps: they still smelt slightly of mongoose. Disguising this smell (I hoped) successfully, I then set traps carefully in two widely separated monkey tunnels in the long grass, being careful not to disturb anything.

Then I started on my doping operation. I took out a good supply of bananas, and chose about one out of every five for the treatment: I made a V-shaped slit, raised the flap, scooped out the soft contents, broke open a nembutal capsule and packed the white powder into the banana, and then pressed the flap down so neatly as to deceive and tempt even the most suspicious of monkeys.

I then scattered these bananas around in fives, each little pile consisting of four innocent and one doped. And in each of those tunnels or monkey runs through the grass I put a doped banana, but beyond the trap, to serve the purpose of a long-stop or second string. I took great care to disturb the grass as little as possible. There remained the question of what to do with my rather obvious nets. I spread them over some bushes beyond the traps and tunnels and the doped bananas, in the hope that some bemused monkey might take his slumber in them, or at least, conveniently close to them.

When all these preparations were completed, we retired to a vantage point high up on the summit side of the clearing, downwind from the traps and fruit; and we awaited developments.

By now it was almost midday. We waited. My hands began

to ache with the weight of my binoculars, and they kept on getting out of focus. Still we waited. Surely this generous distribution of fruit would attract monkeys in quantity! But after two hours there was still no sign of any kind of animal life. My two helpers became restless: they did not fully understand what I was doing, or why we had to be so quiet. Eventually, at four in the afternoon, I let them go back to the vehicle where they could talk without disturbing any potential captures. Left alone, I tried to concentrate, lifting those heavy binoculars to my tired eyes. But only the birds came near me; and soon after six I realised that the night was closing in and that the entire monkey kingdom would now be settling down for the night. So I staggered wearily down the valley and rejoined my sleeping aides, and back we went to the hotel.

One of the directors of the hotel, Mr Seymour-Smith, now displayed the great interest and also the optimism which characterised so many people where the capture of wild animals was concerned – especially thieving animals like monkeys. 'You just want to appear at the back door of this hotel with a banana in your hand,' he suggested; 'you'll soon get any number of Stair's monkeys around you.' I brushed aside this crudely amateurish approach and told him of my own more professional arrangements, also of my early morning climb and my disappointment. 'Well, then,' he said, 'in that case you want to get up at first light and go along to your traps then. The monkeys seem to come down from the summit in the morning and go back in the afternoon. Go in the morning, and you'll probably find them fighting to get into your traps and eat your drugged bananas.'

Cheered by his confidence, I gazed once again, and longingly, at the picture of a Stair's monkey in my reference book – also at my odorous monkey skin: then I sank into an anxious sleep.

I was out of bed at first light, as the director had recommended, and in the damp cold mists of early morning I drove up to my hunting ground, driving at a snail's pace up the

(above) With Paula, a cheetah: 'Let's go for a run.' (centre) 'Whoa, not so fast!' (*below*) With Paula and my Bassett Hound asking: 'How do you run like that?'

Paula plays rugger: (*above*) 'You're offside'; (*below*) but the 'ref'
has not noticed.

twisting and badly graded road that led to my parking place near the beacon. As the light improved I was able to retrace my tracks of the previous evening: water dripped off my hair down my face, and my feet soon became soaked inside my canvas boots as I completed the journey on foot. The mists dispersed, the rising sun shone down the mountain to my level, then down to the telegraph posts and the forest beyond: the animal kingdom began to wake up, and the birds repeated their morning anthems.

At about 6.30 I heard a snapping of twigs from above me, and froze at once into total immobility. The faint crackling sound grew nearer and then turned off to my right, towards the monkey trails and the traps. In high excitement but very cautiously I raised my binoculars: branches were swaying, and here and there I caught glimpses of the back or the long tail of some monkey – of the common vervet or of the Stair's monkey. I couldn't say which. Either way, I trembled with excitement: success appeared to be in sight at last.

Soon, to my delight, I was able to distinguish a small troop of Stair's monkeys. They were feasting upon the fruits of a wild fig tree, and were still on the uphill side of the clearing. This was frustrating: I wanted them to be still hungry when they reached my bananas. After a few minutes, which seemed like hours, they started to come down from the trees and into the tall grass, their heads occasionally lifting and breaking cover in the style of the patas monkey, which lives habitually in long grass. Then, in ecstasy, I heard a noise of wire against metal: a monkey was dashing to and fro in one of my traps! But I controlled my excitement and kept still since I wanted the rest of the troop to stay around and eat those bananas.

There I was disappointed: all too soon I saw them in the trees below the clearing, chattering and climbing away in the most active and wideawake fashion, not looking the least bit dopey. Never mind: at least I had caught one in my trap. So I stumbled and slid down, forgetting the cramp of my long vigil and the wetness of my feet, hurrying in some fear that

D*

the monkey might get away: I could hear the wire platform rattling up and down on the steel base, and too much activity might possibly loosen the locking device.

I parted the grass and looked down; and there, safely inside my trap, I saw not the longed-for Stair's monkey but a blotched genet: it snarled in rage and hatred, and snapped at my fingers when I touched the trap.

Crestfallen, I looked up at the monkeys in the trees, and they looked down at me with deep suspicion, all fully alert, not one displaying any sign of the drug-taker's lethargy. So I studied my bananas, which were rather black by now: they were all untouched. The smaller of the two traps had been sprung, but there was no sort of animal inside: my nets, spread below the clearing, glistened with sunlit dew but were empty. I cursed the genet for upsetting all my careful plans, and went to have a closer look at it.

Blotched genets were not on my list of required specimens. On the other hand, I actually had one; I had caught it myself, and it certainly could be fitted into my collection. I sat down on a cushion of wet grass to work the matter out. I was not a commercial trapper, anxious to catch anything that could be sold. But then again, I was trying to build up a collection of African wild animals. But then once again, I had a conscience in the matter of conservation. I pondered all aspects of the question for some time, but in the end this last consideration proved decisive. Some vervet monkeys frolicked in the trees overhead, and some glossy starlings flew across the forest gap, their violet-blue plumage brilliant in the sun: the beauty and sacredness of wild nature came home to me sharply, and before I could change my mind, I ran to the trap and released the catch. My genet bounded off to freedom.

I hunted out my drugged bananas, feeling rather like a sapper clearing landmines from neutral territory, and then I dug a hole and buried them by an old ant-hill, not wanting them to be unsuspectingly and uselessly eaten by some human or other animal. Then, with great difficulty, I disentangled my nets from the bushes and made two arduous journeys down to the pick-up with all my gear. It had been an unproductive morning from the point of view of my collection, but it had been a worthwhile and memorable experience – a refutation, too, of Captain Boathby's assurance that drugged bananas were an infallible way of catching monkeys.

I spent the next few days there, high in the Vumba Mountains, without adding anything to my collection. My mind was constantly on the Stair's monkey, and all the more so because my book told me that they make excellent pets; I dreamed up many splendid ways of catching them, but never even saw them in the flesh. Then I remembered that they were said to come to the back door of the hotel in search of food. So I tied a long string to the door of an outbuilding, so that I could shut it quickly by remote control, and then laid a long trail of nuts across the yard and into that door, with a big heap of nuts inside to provide the principal bait.

Then I settled down again to the familiar routine of waiting for the Stair's monkey. Eventually, one of them actually turned up, ate the nuts and followed the trail, exactly as I had planned; but when he came to the door of the shed he pushed it, and this tightened the string, over which he immediately tripped and then took fright, making off at once, and abandoning all thought of the alluring nuts within.

From that point on, it was as though the local Stair's monkeys were keeping me under strict surveillance, checking me in and out of the hotel, following my movements just as though I was a potential kidnapper and they were the French police.

And so I went, bumping down the pot-holed road that led for twenty miles, through lush forest and then over undulating green hills, back down to Umtali. I felt a definite respect for my conquerors, and I hoped that the Stair's monkeys felt a corresponding respect for me.

At the Umtali post office I posted that smelly monkey skin off to London, labelling it as 'scientific material'. As I passed the museum, I accelerated and looked the other way:

I did not want to talk about my failure, nor to tease my frustrated self with their captive specimen.

When I arrived back at Douet John was at work on another mongoose cage, stapling on the wire front. He seemed delighted to have me back. The animals appeared to be in good working order: the jackals were snoozing on their bed of freshly cut reeds, and the wild cat had lost none of its dislike for me. I walked over the farmhouse and found Porky blocking the front door, sleeping in the shade: I tickled his ear and he erupted like a volcano, springing up, twitching his tail, snorting angrily. I apologised politely, and he trotted off to settle down again under a flamboyant tree, scratching himself a cool resting place in the dust. Inside the serval cat was passing the time of day by catching the flies on the wire screens. She took no notice of my arrival. The farmhouse was deserted.

At the far end of the verandah I saw an old-fashioned meat safe which had not been there before: it sounded as though there were birds inside. So I came and peered in, and there – perched on a branch near the top of the meat safe – I saw two fledgelings. Of what species could they be? With their downy plumage, their hooked beaks, their yellow legs and feet, they looked rather as though they had been invented by Walt Disney. I thought that they must be some kind of falcon, so I went back to the pick-up and collected my luggage and dug out my copy of Austin Roberts's *Birds of South Africa* and started to leaf through it. But while the book described the fledgelings of various species, the illustrations were all of adult birds. I brooded over various combinations of colour and form, in respect of beaks and legs and plumage and eyes and the rest, and still was no wiser: these little birds might have belonged to any one of a variety of different species.

How little I really knew about natural history! I could recognise any creature of a species that we had in the Jersey Zoo, and many others that I had seen elsewhere. But when suddenly confronted with young birds to identify, I was wholly at a loss, even though a first-class reference book was in my hands.

I was having a bath when the Fallas came back together, and I had to shout through the closed door and the steam to tell them about my recent disappointment. It was a blow for them too: they had been very enthusiastic about my Vumba Mountain trip, and shared my interest in the Stair's monkey.

' "And I too, my lord, have not been idle",' quoted Robin. 'We've got a couple of hawks for you. We can't tell whether they're a pair or not, but you'll know all about that.'

I finished my bath and came out to join them on the verandah, pretending that I hadn't already had a look.

'Mike Smoelke tells us that they're goshawks,' continued Robin. 'What do you think?' Evasively I told him that there were two species of goshawk in that part of Africa, and that we'd be able to identify these two specimens in about a year's time. He then told me that they had got a leveret for me, a young specimen of the Rhodesian bush hare: I didn't really want this for my collection, but I accepted it so as not to dampen their enthusiasm.

It turned out that during my absence the wild-cat kitten had taken a fancy to Roselle, would come up to the front of the cage when she approached and allow itself to be scratched on the back of its head. This was another instance of something that I have noticed elsewhere: young animals will often respond to young people, while still distrusting the adults of our species.

During the evening of the following day I heard music in the distance, a tribal sounding beat of drums and singing across the river. Here, I thought, was the ideal opportunity for me to record some authentic African music. I had brought out from England a very heavy tape-recorder: I now loaded this on to the pick-up and drove down the dirt track to the pumphouse. Here I had to leave the vehicle and proceed silently across a single-plank bridge: I wanted to approach and make my recording without being noticed. If my presence and my intention were to be detected, the performance would either come to an end or else become self-conscious and therefore falsified.

That rhythmical wailing continued, to the accompaniment of massed choirs of frogs and crickets. I pressed on, wishing the tape-recorder wasn't quite so heavy, and wondering why my steady progress seemed to bring me no closer to the music. Here and there the bush had been burned, and black charred roots caught my canvas boots at almost every step. I still pressed on, and the drumming and the chanting never seemed to falter, but continued steadily, with a single voice occasionally calling out some sentence and then being answered by the rest.

Eventually I breasted a small rise and saw the glow and smoke of a fire among some native huts. So I turned off from the path and hid behind a shrub that had survived the fire, attached my microphone and tested the recorder. Its 'magic eye' lit up with interest, visibly responding to the sounds that were being received: I sat back and let the machine do its work.

After twenty minutes or so the tape came to an end and I switched the machine off. It was now time for me to steal away as silently as I had come. But perhaps I was in too much of a hurry: I happened to brush against one of the branches of the shrub that was hiding me and thus dislodged some roosting poultry. At once they clucked and chattered in noisy alarm, left the shrub and ran off to the huts. The drumming and chanting stopped abruptly. I froze in the sudden silence, feeling rather like a schoolboy discovered out of bounds. What could I say to them, how could I explain my presence? Would they think I was a police spy? My heart seemed to be beating as loudly as those now silenced drums, and I felt sure that they would hear it and so find me: I even saw a torch being flashed in my direction. But then I heard some relaxed laughter, and soon a single drum started up again, beating steadily to recall the others to the continuation of the programme.

I stayed behind that shrub for another twenty minutes, so as to be sure of making no further disturbance: then, at a moment when clouds cut off the revealing moonlight, I stole away, back to the path and down to the river and my pick-up. In some relief, and with a great sense of achievement and acquisition, I drove back to the farmhouse. Nightjars would rocket up before the headlights as I drove, always waiting until the last possible moment before taking off.

'Hullo,' said Robin as I came across the stoep, tripping over the solid form of Porky as I did so; 'You've just missed a phone call from Que Que. A farmer wanted to know whether you would be interested in buying a female cape hunting dog from him. He wants you to phone him back in the morning.'

This raised, in urgent form, a question which had been bothering me for some time. The animal collection that was being formed and accommodated in the tobacco barn was growing steadily, and with little effort on my part: it seemed that I only needed to spread the word around, letting people know what species I wanted, and most of them would be offered. But this method of working, added to the task of looking after the growing collection, meant that I had to be on the spot almost continuously. In a way I welcomed this: it was good to be in close contact with animals again, learning the art of looking after them, settling them down in captivity, persuading them to take nourishment.

But all this imposed strict limits upon my movements; and I had plans to travel more widely. For one thing, Gerald Durrell had given me an introduction to Robert and June Kay, who lived with a varied collection of domestic and wild animals in the Okavango swamps of north-western Botswana, then called Bechuanaland. I had corresponded with the Kays, and they had asked me to join them at their camp if Southern Rhodesia failed to give me everything I wanted. This idea appealed to me: I thought that life in those swamps would gratify my urge to get away from twentieth-century civilisation for a time, while also giving me the chance to see plenty of wild life.

So I made up my mind accordingly. I would spend two more months at Douet Farm, collecting 'bush orphans' and small mammals in the Glendale area, and then I would send the whole collection from Salisbury to London by air before travelling on to wilder parts where I could study the wild life, and consider the problems of its conservation, in its natural environment. So I wrote to the Kays and accepted their invitation.

This decision meant that I could collect freely in the meantime, with no fear of being encumbered in my later travels. I knew that the Edinburgh Zoo wanted a pair of hunting dogs; so in the morning I phoned the Que Que number and told the farmer that I would pay him ten pounds for the one he had, and would drive down to collect it on the following Saturday.

I had met these dogs before, when I was soldiering in Northern Rhodesia. They had been aroused by the sound of rifle fire, and I saw their characteristic sharp ears and powder-puff tails above the grass. As we drew nearer they started to prance up and down in excitement, as though they were glad to see us, thus revealing the black and white markings – different in each animal – which varied the basic mustard colour of their coats.

On that occasion they almost seemed to be welcoming us in the manner of domestic dogs. But this appearance of friendliness was deceptive: the cape hunting dog does not like human beings at all, and has great contempt for all domestic dogs, which he hunts down on sight. A fierce species: their hunting tactics are well known in this part of Africa. They gather in large packs and run down the largest game, even old lions, maintaining the pressure steadily: when the lead dogs get tired their place is taken by others, which have saved their strength by cutting corners during the long pursuit. Thus the quarry gets no relief, and will be finally dealt with by specialist killer dogs which always go for the throat. Such a pack will not be deterred by any number of casualties in its ranks: the dead or wounded will be left behind, and the pack will press on remorselessly.

A captive of this breed would need careful top-security accommodation. And so, with John's help, I wired off another stretch of the tobacco barn with some heavy-gauge pig-wire, separating this new enclosure from the jackals' cage by a narrow passage way. The wild cat, the rock monitor, the slender mongoose, the hare and the jackals all watched with deep interest, no doubt wondering what their new companion would be like. I was concerned about John's reaction: he did not recognise the picture of a cape hunting dog that I showed him, but he'd been badly scratched by the wild-cat kitten that morning, and if he got an idea of what was coming he might walk out or demand danger money.

I did not ask John to make a travelling-crate for the hunting dog: instead, I took the jackals' one. My nominal reason for this was my own uncertainty about the size a specially made crate should be: my real reason was the unreliability of any crate made by John, if it was to be used for carrying a beast that could be dangerous. The farmer would have the dog caged already, and we would just have to drive it across into the jackals' crate.

And so on the Saturday we loaded up at first light and set forth, so as to complete the round trip in one day. One diversion, which had aroused my curiosity, was planned. I had told Mike and Winky Smoelke that I was driving to the Que Que area; and they insisted that I should call at the farm of Winky's parents for an early lunch. There (they explained) I would be able to meet Sir Roy. Would this be Sir Roy Welensky, of Central Africa Federation fame? Apparently not. Then who? They wouldn't tell me; and so, frantic to find out, I found myself driving down the two hundred miles to the Fletchers' farm. It was a good tarmac road, and a good vehicle would have appreciated it: my poor old pick-up staggered and panted along so hopelessly that I sometimes thought we'd never get there – never find out about the mysterious Sir Roy, never secure that hunting dog.

But we did arrive. 'Persil,' said Mr Fletcher when we had introduced ourselves, 'go and fetch Sir Roy.' There was a long silence, followed by a kind of squawking sound, and then the gallant knight came bustling into the room. He had a long, curved, and powerful beak, surrounded by red wattling, and his plumage was black: I saw at once that he was a hornbill, and Mrs Fletcher told me, more precisely, that he represented the southern variety of the African ground hornbill. 'We have had him since he was a chick, and he is trained to the gun.' This seemed a surprising claim; but before I could query it, Mr Fletcher demonstrated by picking up a .303 rifle and walking outside. Sir Roy followed him closely, in obvious excitement. 'Now if I were to shoot a pigeon,' said Mr Fletcher, 'Sir Roy would retrieve it for me as efficiently as any labrador retriever.'

This remarkable gun bird was completely tame as far as those people to whom he had been formally introduced were concerned. But he would sometimes attack strangers. The day before I came, an African who had drunk too much *scakian* (a native beer) came staggering through the farm's backyard, was set upon by Sir Roy, lost his balance, fell, and received two nasty thrusts from the hornbill's beak. Mrs Fletcher pulled the bird off and rushed the boy down to the Que Que hospital, and they were now awaiting news of the patient, hoping that their faithful but fierce pet would not have to be put down. If this did have to happen, they said, I could have the remains for my collection.

After lunch I left their farm, and drove for an hour along bumpy, dirt roads and through thin bush to the farm where my hunting dog was waiting for me. At one place I saw an old silver mine, last worked in the 1920s – in a very different Rhodesia – and now deserted. Elsewhere along the road I noticed the strict etiquette among Africans who were on the move: the man always walked in front, carrying a stout stick, while his wife followed some ten yards behind like a true beast of burden, some large load balanced magnificently on her head, a *pikinine* strapped securely to her back, her hands free for balancing purposes.

The Afrikaans farmer greeted me kindly when I arrived, gave me a beer, and told me about the extent of the damage done by hunting dogs in his area. Last year they had accounted for nearly a hundred head of his cattle. I had never guessed that they were the farmer's enemy to this degree: no wonder that they were reckoned as vermin in all cattle ranching areas. But they can be judged less harshly if wider considerations are taken into account: in the wild, such predators serve an ecological purpose by killing off the weaker specimens of their victim species, thus maintaining the quality of the stock.

Why was the farmer keeping this particular hunting dog in captivity? She was useful (he told me) as bait. Each time she came into season she was manhandled into a small wire cage, which was hoisted into the higher branches of a strong tree. A cow would then be sacrificed and the carcase, well laced with arsenic, would be left at the foot of the tree. Left alone, the bitch would soon recover from the fright of being manhandled and would then recommence her mournful high-pitched wailing. This would summon the males of her species from everywhere within a ten-mile radius. Assembled together and unable to reach the bitch, all these dogs would then console themselves by feasting on the poisoned carcase, and would then die wretchedly. Thus the farmer could rid the neighbourhood of these vermin and make a small profit as well, since the Agricultural Division of the Territorial Government gave a bounty of one pound for every tail received.

This bounty could be increased by anybody clever enough to take advantage of the dogs' breeding habits. The bitches, when about to whelp, would separate from the main pack and take refuge in the communal maternity homes maintained by the pack. These were established in disused aardvark workings or porcupine earths, and within them the puppies would be born and would lead a subterranean existence until old enough to join the pack. These nurseries were so carefully chosen that they were hard to discover, but if you did find one, you would receive ten pounds for the nursery as well as another pound for every tail. This farmer told me – with obvious satisfaction – that he had once found one of these earths in use, and had blocked up all the entrances but one with old petrol cans, and had then run a rubber hose from the exhaust of his tractor into the remaining entrance. The occupants, young and mothers alike, were thus gassed with carbon monoxide; and when they dug out the workings to count the numbers they were able to claim bounty on no fewer than thirty tails. It must have been a gruesome sight.

Warned by this somewhat unsavoury story, I followed the farmer to where he kept his captive specimen. She was in a pit-like run, covered over with old netting and some barbed wire: old bones and bits of skin were scattered over the ground, while mounds of faeces in each corner swarmed with flies and bluebottles. It was strange and sad to think of any creature surviving in such surroundings. I looked at her: her bat-like ears twitched as I spoke, and she kept crouching, then running up to the far end of her enclosure, crouching there, then returning again. Perhaps she thought that she was in for another spell of imprisonment in the wire cage. This was clearly visible on top of the wire, and there were bloodstains and patches of hair upon it which told their own story of those nights in the treetop.

The animal's keeper was nowhere to be found, though the farmer sent off messengers to find him: it was Saturday, and he was probably off on one of the popular weekend beer sessions of his people. I asked the farmer if there was anybody else who knew how to handle the bitch. He shook his head. 'But I see you've got some nets on your truck: why don't you net her?'

My heart sank at this prospect; but I didn't want to return to Glendale empty handed and have to make this journey a second time. Rather against my will I had agreed to pay ten pounds for this unfortunate creature, and I was determined to take her away from this living hell, and now.

So I plucked up my courage, wishing that I were less well informed about the habits of this species, and their inbred dislike for people. Putting that unhelpful knowledge out of my mind, I folded and tied my net so as to make a sort of long tunnel or bag, closed at one end, so that if only the animal could be persuaded inside, I could tie up the open end and transfer the lot to my crate.

The farmer seemed unimpressed by my courage and resourcefulness: he watched indifferently while an African unbound some wire fastenings and then folded back part of the roof of the bitch's enclosure, so that I could get in. I waited until she was up at the far end before dropping through on to the earthen floor: net in hand, I stood there in some terror. The bitch glared at me from inflamed eyes, watching every movement I made, crouching in her dark corner. The farmer yawned.

Previously, whenever I had needed to catch an animal in a confined space, I had always made a practice of talking steadily and gently throughout. This bolstered up my own confidence at least; and perhaps the animal concerned did get some idea of being sensible and not attacking me. And so, appealing steadily to the bitch's commonsense and logic, I slowly worked my way along the narrow pit: the mouth of my net was held open by a stick, but even so, it kept catching on litter and roots as I advanced.

The bitch backed as far as she could go; then, choosing her moment, she sprang. I swung the net, but unsuccessfully: she got entangled for a short moment but broke away at once, and ran to the other end of the enclosure – the end I had just come from. I must have panicked a little at the crucial moment: it ought to have been possible to lure her into the net, but at such moments, self-preservation is often the dominant instinct, over-riding the immediate purpose.

There we were, she and I together: the African had prudently fastened the wire ceiling back again. What was going to happen? She could have grabbed a leg or arm of mine, but luckily she had refrained, being perhaps too scared and unconfident. Unless I restored her confidence by repeated and unsuccessful attempts to catch her I might be safe from attack. But I wanted more than mere safety; so I sorted out my net and confronted her once again. She faced me, red tongue hanging out, teeth gleaming. I kept the bottom of the net close to the ground, and tried to extend the sides to fill the whole width of the enclosure so that she would have no way out; but my hands were shaking, and I had to keep swallowing. There was not only hostility upon her face: there was *contempt* as well. Then she came for me; and more in blind self-protection than in good judgement, I flung myself aside and pulled the mouth of the net into the line of her attack, very much in a matador's style. She went past me, just brushing my legs, straight into the net; and as my fall continued, I must have twisted up the mouth of the net without meaning to, but quite effectively. There she was, caught; I twisted the net more tightly round and round, and there wasn't a thing she could do about it. It was a memorable moment.

The African grinned broadly as he helped me out of the pit; even the farmer seemed to have enjoyed the performance, and he opened up the door of the jackals' crate for me. But before putting her inside I thought that this would be a good moment to remove the tight leather collar that had bitten deep into the skin around her neck; so I did this, using an evil looking butcher's knife that I borrowed from the African, and sliding a piece of wood under the collar so as not to cut the skin. This tightened the collar even closer so that the poor beast was nearly choked: when the collar was finally off, she lay back and looked up at me with mournful eyes but doing nothing at all, as though she fully expected to receive the coup de grâce.

There was a nasty sore where the collar had been: if it had been left in place it would have grown tighter as she grew and would probably thus have ended by strangling her. I told the African to fetch a box from the pick-up, and I sprayed the sore with a chloromycetin antibiotic spray and packed sulphanilamide powder into the wound. Then I up-ended the travelling crate with the door open and hung the net inside it, let it unwind, and finally cut the binding: the bitch slipped out and was safely in the crate.

I thanked the farmer and the African for their help, paid my ten pounds, and started off on the drive back to Glendale, feeling flushed with success. On the way I stopped for a sundowner with the Fletchers, and heard that Sir Roy had been granted a reprieve and that therefore the African ground hornbill would not be added to my collection.

It was late when I came back to Douet Farm, and I decided to leave my hunting dog in her cage until the morning. So I topped up her water trough and went over to the farmhouse. Robin was waiting up for me, glass in hand, full of curiosity about my day. So I embarked upon the epic story of my struggles in the pit; but I was so tired that I fell asleep, in one of Robin's warm enveloping armchairs, in the middle of the conversation.

CHAPTER 4

To England with Love

I COULD not free my mind of the fate that lay in store for me:
within a week I was due to deliver my talk to the local farming
community. With this serious distraction, thanks to not keeping
my mind on what I was doing, I very nearly let the jackals
escape. Too preoccupied to learn from this I then – within an
hour or two – actually did give the rock monitor a chance to
escape, which he promptly seized. I wanted to clean out his
cage, so I tied him up in a hessian sack, not realising the
strength of his jaws: when I turned to release him I was too
late. There was a large hole in the side of the sack, and no
monitor. I looked suspiciously at the jackals and the cape hunting dog, but saw no monitor tail protruding from those greedy
mouths, nor any look of satisfied repletion. He was gone.

This piece of carelessness made me feel guilty and foolish;
and to restore my confidence I searched among the large
boulders that were scattered behind the farmhouse, and succeeded in catching three more specimens of the slender mongoose. These, lodged in the tobacco barn, further increased a
carnivorous smell that was already too powerful and was
upsetting my bush hare, causing it to twitch its nose in continual worry. So I removed all four mongooses to a toolshed
nearby.

Saturday came, and the sun set with dark sombre haste:
when zero hour arrived, I launched myself into the talk as a
cabaret artist into an act. At times I found myself getting out of
my depth and had to change the subject hurriedly, and in

70

How we lived and travelled: (*above*) base camp on the west bank of the Thamalakane River, Okavango; (*below*) the Kays' DUKW, Okavango Swamps.

Vultures: (*above*) my 'first'; (*below*) releasing one too many.

general, I did flit from one subject to another: the economic use of ungulate fauna outside game reserves; the social life of marmosets in captivity; the futility of game slaughter as a means of tsetse-fly control. But what with one thing and another, I managed to keep going.

Question time came, and I was let off lightly. There was one middle-aged school-teacher, well versed in the ways of birds and bees, who commented upon the fact that I was sending home a female cape hunting dog with no mate. 'How do you expect it to breed?' No offer of a male hunting dog was then forthcoming, but a slim weatherbeaten farmer in the second row said: 'Would you be interested in a pair of serval cats?' I gulped. 'More than words can express!' What a question! It was like asking a ship-wrecked sailor if he'd be interested in a flaxen-haired beauty.

I went home to Douet with this offer in mind, after the evening had ended in general sociability. Now that it was safely over, my ordeal did not seem so very terrible: back at the farm, I was able to relax over those refreshments and drinks, enjoying my company and the sense of being an admired and successful lecturer.

In the morning I went over to the tobacco barn and found John shuffling around as usual. He grinned cheerfully, but ceased to grin when I told him about the newly expected arrivals – two bigger versions of Romeo, I explained, pointing at the wild cat to which I had given that name. John swallowed in dismay. It was rather petty of me, perhaps, to tease him about the fierceness of our animals; on the other hand, I had heard from the boss boy of the farm that he often boasted to the other Africans about the perilous deeds of his daily routine. He might welcome any alarming talk that helped to foster this image.

Soon I was off. A winding strip of road took me through some attractive hilly bushland; it was strewn with kopjes, and these were studded with gigantic boulders which looked as smooth as facecream. My destination was Combe Farm, which was fifteen miles to the north-west of the small farming centre of Banket: I could hardly get there quickly enough, in my anxiety

E

to get hold of those serval cats before the offer was withdrawn.

Mr Shattock invited me into his farmhouse with the usual Rhodesian hospitality, and over a cup of china tea he told me how these two serval cats had been found on his farm, orphaned, during the previous year. He and his wife had brought them up indoors until they had become so boisterous that they could no longer be trusted with the children.

They were being kept in an overgrown tennis court, which could hardly have been played on for some years since within the wired enclosure shrubs and undergrowth were growing freely. The farmer told me that there would be no need for a net this time: he would be able to pick up the male, and his wife would be able to pick up the female. 'They are very tame,' he explained, 'I once tried releasing them to fend for themselves, with the idea that they might possibly do an Elsa on us, but they were too trusting, and I nearly lost Tammy – that's the female – to some Kaffir dogs. The male is called Teja, which means "beware" in the Biyla language of Northern Rhodesia.'

I took my station by the entrance of this overgrown tennis court, with my travelling-crates held ready: I was glad not to have to use the nets again, since it is sad to see elegant wild animals entangled and helpless, with all their pride destroyed. The Shattocks went inside and called for their respective pets. 'Teja mern, come here, Teja mern!' called Mr Shattock in true native tones, while his wife chanted, 'Tammy, Tammy, Tammy!': it was as though they were competing for a prize. But five minutes went by, and still neither cat had put in an appearance. Perhaps they knew what was in store. 'I know what,' said Mr Shattock, 'I'll go and shoot a pigeon.' He was back very quickly: some pigeon must have been standing by in self-sacrificing readiness. Teja must have scented blood: he broke cover, and surprised me by being the largest serval cat I had ever seen. He had a shoulder height of some twenty inches.

He walked confidently over to his master, who picked him up and tossed the dead pigeon into one of the travelling boxes and then put Teja by the door. He fell for it, and walked in at once, so that I was able to close the door gently behind him.

Tammy was not going to be fooled so easily. She also had scented blood and emerged from the undergrowth, standing straight upon her long legs, her short tail twitching, her large bright eyes gazing upon her mistress inquisitively. But when Mrs Shattock bent down to stroke her and then pick her up, she sprang aside: she had probably heard her husband spitting and cursing in his box, and in a moment she was off into the deep jungle of the tennis court. But another shot was fired and another pigeon brought down, and Tammy reappeared as though that bang was the dinner gong: when the second bird was put into the second box, she too sprang upon it and was secured.

I stowed the boxes on the back of the pick-up, made my farewells, and went. I could not help feeling a certain guilty compassion. These wild and noble beasts were going to live in pampered and secure circumstances, more comfortably (in most senses) than they could ever hope to live in the wild. Even so, the prospect immediately before them was a totally incomprehensible experience of imprisonment and travel: they were going to suffer – for a time – very much as a young conscript suffers during his first bewildering days in the army.

There were now ten days to go before this collection was due to be shipped to England; and the housing of these cats presented a problem. Servals are great climbers, and an open enclosure would not do: furthermore, I did not want them to fight the jackals or the hunting dog through the wire. Fortunately the Smoelkes came to my rescue: at their farm, some twenty minutes' drive from Douet, they had a large clean outbuilding, with a big window and – half-way up the wall – a concrete ledge. They put this accommodation at my cats' disposal: I arranged for some long grass to be cut as a floor covering, and I brought the two crates inside.

It would be a welcoming gesture, I thought, and a help to their happy establishment in this new temporary home, if I shot them a pigeon each. So out I went with a borrowed .22 rifle, and spent half an hour trying to do what Mr Shattock had done in a moment. The trouble was that I am not a very good shot: in my army days, I had never done well on the rifle-range. I also knew that it was considered unsporting to shoot a sitting bird. So I found some sitting pigeons and shouted at them, and when they flew away I followed them with the rifle-sights and fired. By this means I brought down just one feather. So I reminded myself that nature is cruel anyway, put aside my sporting instincts, crept upon sitting birds and shot them successfully. As I carried the two carcases to the servals I apologised to them, explaining that it was in the good cause of kindness to fellow creatures.

Even with a good meal offered I found that the servals refused to come out of their crates in my presence. I left them there in the shed, thanked the Smoelkes, and went back to Douet, to find John looking scared out of his wits and one of the jackals crouching in the corner of the barn. Apparently he had been giving them some fresh water and went into their enclosure without fastening the wire door properly: the jackal had not attacked him but had started to run around in alarm and had thus escaped into the open barn. John had managed to get between it and the barn door, but when he tried to drive it back into its pen, it had just bared its teeth and uttered a low-pitched growl. This was quite enough for John: he stayed by the door in mounting terror until I came. Seeing itself outnumbered, the jackal then slunk back into its pen and John could get away to safety.

I was up early the next morning, anxious to drive over before breakfast and see whether the serval cats had settled down sufficiently to eat the pigeons. I peered in through the grimy glass of the shed window, and there was the male, sitting on the concrete ledge and hissing at me angrily. Tammy, I thought, must still be in one of the crates; but when I went into the shed – very carefully – she was nowhere to be seen. I couldn't believe it: I had locked the door, she hadn't escaped as I came in, the window did not open, there was no other exit. I ran up to the farmhouse to ask the Smoelkes if they had needed to take Tammy out for some reason: no, they hadn't. We went back to the shed and examined it again more carefully; and this time, we found a wooden panel at the back, under the concrete ledge, which would open if pushed at top or bottom.

So Tammy had escaped. I wondered what I would say to the Shattocks: they would despise my incompetence and feel sympathy for poor widowed Teja. But Mike Smoelke was encouraging: he thought that Tammy wouldn't have gone far from the mate to whom she had been married so long and so happily.

So for the next few hours I crashed about in the shrubbery and bush around the shed and then further afield, often tripping over, but never seeing anything in the least like a serval's spoor. So I took the Smoelkes' advice: having kept servals themselves, they knew their ways. They thought that Tammy would come back to Teja under cover of darkness, and probably at dawn the next day: we would organise a search then, but in the meantime they would watch out for her during the day. So I went back to Douet with a promise to return at half past five next morning, half expecting to find further escapes from the tobacco barn, relieved therefore when all its occupants were safely at home and apparently in good spirits.

In the morning, I was met in the Smoelkes' drive by two Africans and a number of thin disreputable looking dogs. Mike then came out with his pedigree dalmatian, which looked upon its canine company in aristocratic disdain, and we all went round behind the farmhouse to the shed. The two Africans and their dogs went round to the left and we went round to the right: the idea was to join forces behind the shed and to cut off two lines of retreat if Tammy happened to be lurking in the undergrowth.

The daylight was just peeping through the blue gum trees, and a thin layer of ground mist enveloped the dogs. As we came round we heard them barking excitedly as though in hot pursuit of something: we could see their tails waving about the mist, and we followed eagerly, hoping that they had not merely flushed a rabbit or something similar. They closed in on one of the blue gum trees and clustered around it, barking and leaping: I looked up the tall trunk and there was Tammy, clinging for all she was worth.

I quickly told the two Africans to take their dogs away: if Tammy had fallen among them – and she seemed about to fall – they would be almost certain to attack her. Then I spread out my net, which I had wisely brought with me, and Mike and I held it out under the tree, just as though we were firemen under a burning building. The dalmatian was told to sit down and did so, downwind of the net, from which there came a rich bouquet of varied animal smells which plainly intrigued him. Then Tammy's hind legs started to lose their grip, thus increasing the load upon her front claws: her lynx-like tail, some thirty feet above us, twitched, and she started to slip and fall, sliding and scratching, but very soon ending up in our net.

There she was easy to manage, being exhausted by the chase and the climb: we lifted her gently and took her back to the shed. Teja growled and hissed and spat by way of welcome, and indeed took angry steps towards us: we put Tammy on the ground and left them. Then, through the window, we saw Teja go up to his mate and start to lick her face gently, occasionally glaring up at us. Tammy was still panting, and a small trickle of blood came from her mouth: she must have hurt herself slightly while falling or in the net. Teja tended this small wound, fussing over her like a devoted and attentive husband, and soon Tammy rolled over, stood up shakily, and went across to lap slowly at the water dish.

I felt wonderfully relieved: it was like unexpectedly good fortune in love. I wanted to thank everybody. I patted the dalmatian gratefully, and gave the Africans beer money on an exaggerated scale – it was more like vintage port money – begging them to give their helpful dogs some extra rations, though without much hope that this would actually happen.

The bonds between animals are often stronger and more binding than the bonds of friendship and matrimony between humans. It was only because of the close bond between

Tammy and Teja that they were now together again. I hoped that when they had settled down in England, this same bond would make their marriage fruitful as well as happy, and that kittens would be born which would not have to suffer this very damaging kind of dislocation in early life.

Robin was delighted with my news, and suggested that since in the event Tammy had come to no harm, there was no need to tell the Shattocks about the episode. I agreed. It is extremely disappointing if you entrust a pet to somebody and then learn that it has been allowed to escape. I remember once, at the dog kennels in Surrey, greeting two people who were going to leave their pekinese for a fortnight's stay. While they were explaining their pet to me, and telling me that he needed to have chicken and rabbit on alternate days, we were interrupted by shouts from one of the kennel-maids: an alsatian had escaped from the exercise paddock. 'Back in a minute,' I shouted, and ran off in pursuit. I was back twenty minutes later, leading that ungrateful dog by my tie, but the pekinese and its owners had gone without even leaving a note or message. This was rude but understandable: how could they trust an establishment from which pets were able to get away?

By this later stage of my stay in Rhodesia the news had penetrated to the more distant parts of the locality that I would purchase any kind of animal that anybody was able to catch and offer. In actual fact I wasn't quite so undiscriminating in my requirements, and I was somewhat disconcerted at the variety of the birds and small mammals that were brought to the farm, with even the occasional reptile. So I tried to make it clear all round that I was only interested in certain species. But I didn't want the rejected offerings to be cooked and eaten, so I released them among the boulders behind the farmhouse – possibly repopulating the farmland thereby with species that it had not seen for many a long year.

One wizened old Mdala, who looked as though he had been journeying for a week or so to meet me, came and produced a small green snake from a cigarette box. Casually, without thinking, I touched the snake. It had been one of those really hot days, and for the last three hours I had been tiring myself in another attempt to catch some of those rainbow-coloured lizards: the only thought in my mind was that the collection would – after all – acquire some kind of reptile that day.

The old man had come a long way so I caused his face to light up with a generous payment. Then, for want of a safer place, I put the cigarette box in the glove compartment of my pick-up, and went into the house to consult my reference books. I didn't want to lose face with John by ignorance of what kind of snake it was. After careful consideration, I identified it – to my considerable alarm – as a striped skaap-steker, which is the Afrikaans for 'sheep-killer': a poisonous species, or semi-poisonous at least. I had broken an elementary rule. The wise man never handles a snake without finding out what species it is.

I went over to the tobacco barn to collect one of the small plywood boxes which I had originally intended for frogs. John offered to help, but hastily withdrew the offer when I told him that I was going to collect a poisonous snake.

I went back to the pick-up, opened the door very carefully, and looked inside the glove compartment. The box was there, open, but with no snake to be seen. I threw myself out of the cab hurriedly, as though there was a hand grenade inside: then, feeling rather like a timid woman in the reptile house at the zoo, I peered in through the windscreen and the side windows, searching every corner in sight, but finding no sign of any sheep-killer. So I opened the door nervously and lifted the seat-cushion, but there was only some odd bits of rubbish beneath it. I poked at this with a stick: still no snake. I felt even so that it was probably somewhere in the cab, since the windows had been closed; this made me reluctant to drive the pick-up, so I left it with both doors open and borrowed Robin's Land-Rover for my evening visit to the servals. If the snake was still around perhaps it would take the hint and go.

Reay Smithers managed to find me a mate for the female cape hunting dog, since a museum had just offered him one for five pounds. This was a stroke of luck for me and (I thought) for the female too: she had wagged her tail and tried to play when one of the farm dogs had come up close to the pig-wire of her run, and I felt sure that she would be glad to have a companion of her own kind. On this basis I replanned the travelling arrangements, asking John to make a large crate in which these two could travel together.

Then I went to the museum to collect the male. He looked very frightened, and when I pressed my face to the wire door to get a better look he cringed back into the corner of his box, his large ears flattened down. I took him back to the tobacco barn, intending to put him in with his new girl friend, so that they could get used to each other before they started on their long journey to Edinburgh. But when I manoeuvred the crate into the wire enclosure I was sorry to find the female growling at the new arrival from her corner, and not showing any of the signs of friendship that she had shown to the farm dog. I opened up the crate and had to tip it up to get the dog out: the female flew at him at once and there was a short scuffle which ended with his abject submission, his lady love standing over him victoriously. This fight made the jackals very excited, and they ran around their enclosure yelping, their dorsal hairs standing almost on end; by contrast, the young hare went almost frantic with anxiety, his eyes glazing over; so I took his cage away from the commotion.

One of my wire traps, baited with the usual selection of mixed foods – raw egg, meat, grain, fruit – now caught another rock monitor. At first I thought he was the one which got away, but when I looked closer I saw that this one had quite a different facial expression: he also responded very differently to my friendly overtures. I was careful not to put him in a hessian sack, and he became quite tame before long, developing a passion for duck eggs.

The serval cats were eating well by now, though they stuck to pigeons and refused to touch the raw meat I offered them daily. My shooting therefore had to improve, and did: in front of Mike Smoelke I actually shot a bird in flight. I had difficulties, however, in keeping the shed clean: if I came in unprotected, Teja would attack me at once, and the only thing he respected was a net, which I therefore held in front of me, matador-style, whenever I entered the hut. This drove both cats up on to the concrete shelf, from which they would spit and hiss at me while I cleaned up the previous day's leavings of meat, replenished the water, and changed the soiled grass.

Time was now running out, and I needed to think about packing and transport. On a previous visit to Salisbury I had gone around the confectionary shops asking for large tins of the sort used to package biscuits or sweets. I explained that I wanted them to keep a collection of frogs and toads in: I would line them with moss and other vegetation, and thus they would remain damp enough for those amphibians to live in. Now I went back to collect my tins, and those shop-keepers had certainly taken trouble on my behalf: there were ten times as many as I could use, but I didn't like to refuse any of them. So when I drove back down Jameson Avenue to Mazoe Road, it was in a pick-up loaded high with brightly coloured tins, rattling horribly; and when I came to the rough strip roads I had to slow down to a walking pace unless I was to lose both my hearing and my sanity.

I returned to Douet, to find an unexpected addition to the collection: one of my traps, set in hopes of a slender mon-goose, had caught a female cape pouched mouse instead. I had not thought of having any sort of mouse, but then, I'd never met this kind before. She was unbelievably tame. I picked her out of the trap by the end of her pink stubby tail, set her down in my hand, and stroked her mottled grey-black coat: her nose twitched in appreciation of this new sensation, and she was soon nibbling at some bread. I took her into the farmhouse to show the children, who were charmed: the goshawks, in their cage on the stoep, were charmed as well, but in a different way – they looked at the little mouse hungrily. I found Mrs Tittlemouse a home in one of the smaller sweet-tins, having first punctured the lid for air and given her some wood shavings for bedding.

On the last evening but one before the collection was to depart, I packed some of the larger tins with cotton wool and moss, making sure that it was thoroughly damp. Then I took John with me and drove down to a flooded area of the Mazoe River, where each night the noise of the amphibians was almost deafening. Wearing some outsize wellington boots that I had borrowed from Robin, with a canvas bag attached to my army belt and a powerful torch in my hand, I splashed about in the moonlight, grabbing at frogs and toads with varying degrees of success, and putting the ones that I did catch into the canvas bag. John watched in silence, with the air of a man who's just had final proof of something that he's suspected for a long time: crazy or not, I kept at it, transferring my captives to the moist and mossy tins whenever the canvas bag started to get full. Some slithered out of my hands, or leapt from the tin before I could get the lid on, but I persevered until I had some fifty specimens. There were a mixed bunch, and I had no notion what species were included: there would be time later for classifying them.

The last days of any collection are hectic: there is so much that cannot be done before the last moment, since animals must stay in their travelling-crates for the shortest possible time. Cages have to be made absolutely secure, water containers have to be devised so as not to spill in transit, and food has to be provided to last the animal for a period of twice the anticipated time of travelling.

Tammy was the first animal to be crated. I put a pigeon into one of the crates, and being either hungrier or bolder than Teja, she went straight in and was secured. At six in the morning on the day of departure I went in to catch Teja also, and had to use a subtler trick: I held the net in front of me and advanced towards the shelf, under which he was crouching, pushing the crate forwards with my foot as I came. He could thus see my foot *through* the cage, and he sprang upon it, thus landing inside the cage, which was immediately closed upon him. Even a double lock upon the door was not quite enough to reassure John as we drove back to Douet.

During the previous evening I had put the jackals' and the hunting dogs' crates into their respective cages, in the hope that they would get used to them overnight: I might even find them already inside. But now, unfortunately, I saw that the opposite had happened: all four animals were sitting as far as possible from their crates, looking very suspicious, and all the more so when I began my preparations. I went into the hunting dogs' enclosure, making sure that John fastened the door behind me, and carrying a net for protection: as with Teja, I then tried to manoeuvre the heavy crate across the floor with my foot, towards the two animals which were now crouching angrily. The female leapt, but on top of the crate, not into it: I talked to them both very soothingly, begging them to go quietly, pointing out that there were big steaks of horse-meat inside. And so, slowly, I got within striking distance of the male, pushed the box forward sharply, trapped him inside, up-ended the box and fastened it securely.

The trouble was that the female was supposed to travel in that same box: I would have to catch her in another crate and then transfer her. I tried this, using the original jackal box, but it soon became clear that she didn't intend to be caught as easily as her husband. At this point Robin came in, and gave me another of his pearls of wisdom. 'Chase the damn thing with the monitor,' he said, 'she'll soon get into the crate to get away from it.' I wasn't at all anxious to handle the rock monitor, but time was getting short, and I had to leave for Salisbury soon. So Robin grabbed the monitor out of his box as casually as if he had been handling reptiles all his life, and passed it over the netting to me. The female hunting dog looked alarmed at the introduction of this new and unfair weapon, and when I advanced upon her, holding the monitor in front of me like a gun, she backed nervously into the box, just as Robin had expected. She wasn't the only nervous one: the monitor had been wriggling in my hand and scratching my arm with its sharp hind claws, and I was glad when I could put it safely away.

All this had been too much for John, and he had gone.

Robin and I managed to decant the female into the travelling-crate with her mate easily enough, but with a certain amount of noise, which brought a gathering of inquisitively grinning Africans around the door of the tobacco barn. They scattered, however, when we suggested that one of the hunting dogs was still loose.

The trickiest part of the operation was now over. The jackals gave no trouble: they must have been watching the hunting dog episode carefully and anxiously, since when I merely showed the monitor to them – from outside their enclosure – they took the point at once and got into the safety of their crate.

Romeo – the African wild-cat kitten – was already in his travelling cage, and the four slender mongooses, the chameleons, the hare and the pouched mouse were already in theirs. I checked everything carefully, and made some more air-holes in the tins of the frogs and toads. My last task was that of crating the two young goshawks: I decided to line the wire walls of their travelling-cage with hessian so that they could not catch their feathers in the wire. When I started to remove the two birds from the safety of their cage for transfer, the farm's pet serval cat went almost wild with excitement, thinking her great moment had come. We had to shut her up until the job was done.

We now stacked all these cages on the pick-up, with the heavier ones at the bottom and the whole lot just about managing to balance safely. Roselle said a tearful goodbye to Romeo, and indeed Romeo looked genuinely upset at having to become estranged from his admirer: Porky, less well mannered, ran off in terror at the barking of the hunting dogs, and took refuge on the familiar verandah. Robin banged on the roof of the cab by way of farewell to my collection, Pris and James waved from the shade of the farmhouse, the jackals wailed like bagpipes, and we were off.

In Salisbury John and I had to wait for the veterinary office to open before we could get the necessary health certificates. While we waited an inquisitive crowd gathered, and we had a hard task to stop them from pulling back the hessian from the cages and even climbing on top of the load. The more noise the animals made, the bigger the crowd grew, and I was glad when an African policeman arrived to turn them back.

Eventually the office opened, and a veterinary surgeon came out to give the animals a close inspection. Romeo just missed his fingers when the hessian was lifted up, and one of the servals also tried to attack him: he decided to call it a day, and issued a comprehensive health certificate forthwith.

Then I had to get an export permit from the Game Department; this was quickly done, and then we could drive out to the airport. Here I found that the customs forms had not been completed, as the airline authorities had promised: this meant another hour of filling in forms, in the middle of which I was interrupted by a journalist who wanted a full account of the collection. Then each crate had to be weighed and loaded into the aircraft under my anxious eyes, with careful stipulations about which crates were to be put together and which were not; and the airline's animal attendant had to be briefed about the individual needs of every animal.

I knew they would be all right: I had cabled the time of their arrival at Heathrow to the zoo representative in England, and I knew that they would be looked after on arrival by the RSPCA hostel at the airport. Even so, it was not easy to part. I went from crate to crate, growing more and more miserable as I said so many successive farewells; and when I finally took my leave of the attendant I did so most reluctantly. He was my last link with the collection into which I had put so much of my time and energy and devotion.

And so, sadly, John and I left the airport alone. These last two months had been a remarkable experience for me: I had learned an enormous amount about the animal kingdom, and the difficulties that animals meet when their wild native habitat is turned into farmland. In a sense man and beast are always at war, but the war intensifies when economic issues are involved, and many animals are then destroyed, often in ignorance, often quite pointlessly. Conservation is most necessary: this fact is shown by the vast stretches of Rhodesian bush through which I travelled without seeing any signs of wildlife.

Fortunately, the Rhodesian Game Department is progressively minded and does much towards creating animal sanctuaries and other conservationist measures, such as the Wankie Game Reserve and the newly created Lake McIlwaine Park. But such measures are of little value unless they are backed up by an awareness among the people generally of the importance of conservation; and this is chiefly a matter of education, since people seldom give serious thought to a problem that does not confront them personally in daily life.

Education is indeed the main thing, but money comes into the picture too. As we drove away from the airport, I thought of how useful it would be if Porky – the very endearing bush pig of Douet Farm – were to be employed as a flag seller in the streets, pestering people to buy his little flags, raising money for the cause of wildlife conservation. He'd raise a lot.

CHAPTER 5

Lions, Hens and Spaniels

IT was now time for me to leave Southern Rhodesia for the next stage of my expedition, which was to take me into the country now called Botswana, then the British Protectorate of Bechuanaland. John and I left Salisbury in the pick-up, heading for Francistown in that country.

On the way I stopped to spend a weekend in Bulawayo and make good any deficiencies in my kit, with a view to the new problems which would be created by life in the swamps. This city had hardly changed at all since my Rhodesian Army days, when I had spent some five months in the Llewellyn Barracks at nearby Heany. It is a more mellow city than Salisbury, its architecture much less modernised; its heavily cambered highways, originally laid out so that a U-turn could be made within their width by a waggon and its four oxen, still retain the same width, giving the city a spacious uncongested character. Wandering in those broad streets among those old houses, I could easily imagine what the life there must have been like for the early settlers at the turn of the century.

I sat back to read my Sunday newspaper, and was very disconcerted to find myself and my activities made into a major news item. There was a bold headline: THIS WEEK A FLYING ZOO TOOK OFF FROM SALISBURY. Then the article followed: 'Mr Mallinson should right now be somewhere out in the wilds of the Okavango Swamp region of Bechuanaland Protectorate: lean, bronzed, going after his quarry with the

(*left*) With a Collared Peccary at Jersey Zoo;

(*right*) trade both ways – Pufelli's (my European red fox) first view of Africa from the *Warwick Castle*.

A vulture tucked underneath my arm.

age-old excitement of the hunter out in the open, but with the added zest of knowing that what he is doing is infinitely worthwhile.' The writer couldn't leave it at that: 'How many Rhodesians,' he went on, 'must envy these fortunate characters who come out to Africa on assignments to film our wildlife or collect specimens for Zoos, and disappear on safari for months. He may of course be swatting mosquitoes as I write this, and wishing to high heaven that he, too, was somewhere in a city within reasonable distance of a long cool one with ice chinking in the glass. But for all that, I'd still like to be with him, and I am aware of no small degree of envy. Good luck to you, Mr Mallinson, as yours is the kind of "hunting" that warrants a salute.'

This is the kind of thing that happens when you get into the clutches of the press. Feeling an urgent need to get away and out into the wilds, I drove rather fast down the last stretch of Rhodesian tarmac to the border town of Plumtree, and then over the bumpy earthen roads of Bechuanaland to Francistown.

We arrived there in baking heat, the temperature being well up in the nineties. I parked the exhausted pick-up in the shade of a fig tree so that it could cool off a little, gave John half a crown with instructions to be back in two hours, and set out to explore the place. The dusty pavement was mostly overshadowed by the corrugated iron verandahs of the shops and houses: I picked my way among them and eventually found an eating place which gave me an uninspired sort of lunch, which needed to be washed down with plenty of iced beer. As seen from this shanty-town hotel, in this midday silence and under this intense heat, Francistown looked like the ideal setting for a Western: I half expected that cowboys would come riding wildly into town with a blaze of six-guns in all directions.

A big man like a mastiff sat beside me at the lunch table, shovelling his food down greedily; so I asked him the best way of getting to Maun, my next destination, which lies on the edge of the Okavango Basin. 'What's yer got?' he asked

F*

between mouthfuls. I told him about the pick-up, admitting its limitations, but explaining that it always seemed to get there in the end. He stopped eating and looked at me in amazement. 'If I was in yer shoes, mate,' he said, 'I wouldn't even bother to start.'

This was hardly encouraging. I paid for my lunch and set out to get a second opinion from a garage. But the only garage was shut until three; so I went back to the pick-up, waited twenty minutes until John came, drove back to the garage, and waited endlessly until it opened.

Around mid-afternoon a European mechanic turned up. 'Do you see any reason why I shouldn't drive this to Maun?' I asked. He looked casually at the pick-up and told me that I had to be joking. 'The police wouldn't even allow you to point a thing like that in the direction of Maun. If you're thinking of driving it there, you can just forget it.'

Reluctantly I accepted this expert opinion and arranged to leave the pick-up at the garage until my return from the swamps. Very fortunately I was not immobilised by this decision: I was told that Riley's Transport trucks ran twice a week to Maun, and that one was leaving that very evening.

I went to see what I was in for. It turned out to be a big diesel truck, its back covered by a canvas awning: the bonnet was open and the engine was steaming, and a fair-sized crowd of Africans was gathered around the back. Among them was a character touting tickets, so I bought two for myself and for John and our luggage: the ticket made it clear that I travelled entirely at my own risk. Then I had the task of stowing on board my three cases, my two wire traps and my tape-recorder; this was not easy, since the truck was already piled high with cargo of every kind, from galvanised dustbins to bags of onions, with less than four feet of clearance between all this stuff and the canvas roof. I got in and crawled around and eventually stowed my luggage, and even managed to level out a flat six feet of space on top of some packing-cases, on which I could lay out my sleeping-bag. I can sleep anywhere, provided that I can stretch out fully; so now, with two hours to go, I tried to catch up on the sleep that I had lost during the journey down from Bulawayo.

I woke up, slightly refreshed and rather disconcerted by the quantity of people and equipment that still had to be found travelling space. There were many Africans, with John very much established by now as one of their crowd, and they all seemed to have bundles of clothing, pots and pans, grimy blankets, angry chickens, commodities of every kind. Somehow the miracle took place, and everything and everybody was stowed, though I forfeited some of the space which I had enjoyed earlier: there were grins all round and a general atmosphere of goodwill.

Twenty minutes later the truck's diesel engine roared into vibratory life: the truck shuddered, the dustbins rattled, the bruised onions gave forth their savour. We moved off, and everything shook and settled down: soon I found myself wedged between two big piles of canned beer in crates, and when I eased myself clear I found that my sleeping-bag kept sliding down into the cracks between the various items of loose cargo. After some experiment I discovered a more or less stable position: it depended upon my keeping my knees wedged against one of the tubular steel supports of the roof.

So, congestedly, we moved on. According to the map, this was a 'secondary' road: when I peered out from under the green tarpaulin, it looked to me more like a rough track of sand and stone, and it was certainly rough. We were shaken up and rearranged incessantly. Even so, John and his African friends managed to sleep in the most remarkable and constantly changing positions: legs tucked beneath them, hands clutching the steel framework of the roof, bodies twisted. I began to suffer from cramp: human pressure around my feet prevented any comfortable stretching. I began to think nostalgically about my bus journey down through Tanganyika and Northern Rhodesia: this seemed rough at the time, but now in retrospect it seemed like luxury.

There were many stops on the way; and just before the sun

disappeared over the dusty dry horizon of the northern Kalahari, we made our eleventh and major stop. The engine was switched off for a well-earned rest, and all the passengers sorted themselves out, extracted their limbs from each other and from the cargo, and jumped out on to the ground, taking their cooking pots with them. Soon small fires were burning beside the sandy track, newspaper parcels were opened and mealie-meal taken out, tea was brewed. I was offered some of the mealie-meal, but declined politely: instead, I wandered down to an empty river, which had just a few stagnant pools where – at the right season – there would be a torrent. The rains had broken already, but it would be months before a river of this seasonal sort became more than pools and a trickle.

Ploughing on through the night and through the loose sand, leaving a trail of swirling sand behind us: the sun rose eventually, rosy in the east, and before eight it was already quite hot. One of the cockerels in the truck kept up a steady crow of complaint.

Before long we were travelling through a more thickly vegetated country, and soon we arrived at the Thamalakane River, which is the eastern border of the Okavango swamps: its crystal-clear waters and the lush greenery of the riverside were lovely to behold, and I reflected upon the ecstasy that they must have given to such early explorers as Selous, arriving here after crossing the dry lands of the Kalahari.

There was a crude bridge over the Thamalakane: vertical stakes and cross-poles, all boarded in and filled with rubble, with just a few square gaps through which the water could pass. There was no barrier, nothing to save a vehicle which wandered off its very narrow track: when our heavy truck drove across, the whole thing creaked.

Seven miles further on, we arrived at Maun, a tribal and administrative centre and my destination. There was nobody to meet me, and I was glad of this: I must have looked more like a dilapidated gipsy than like a keen young British naturalist. John looked comparatively fresh: he was used to this sort of travel and could take it in his stride. He collected my luggage and I went to the small hotel for a shave and a shower. It was a very primitive shower. I thought nostalgically of the motoring trip through the Swiss Alps which I had enjoyed some eight months earlier, and I tried not to think about the fact that, sooner or later, I would have to go back to Francistown under the same awful conditions.

Robert and June Kay were encamped some way down the river, and we were driven out there by a member of the Veterinary Department. The track ran along the cool riverside, winding its way among fallen trees and patches of boggy ground. Soon I saw a copse of impressive fig trees on our right, and three spaniels and a white bull terrier came out to meet us, barking and wagging their tails. 'You've come to a proper menagerie here,' said the veterinary officer, and before I could think of a reply the Kays were welcoming us. They called off their overwhelmingly friendly dogs, and we moved off into the cool shade of the fig trees and made mutual introductions.

I looked around with interest. Among the trees I saw the bulky form of a DUKW, or amphibious vehicle, adapted by the Kays for their travels in the swamp-lands. Nearby, in the open centre of the copse, stood their living tent, its canvas verandah serving as a dining room: freshly cut water reeds covered the ground so as to keep the dust down, the chairs were covered with animal skins, and a Basuto drum added to the bush atmosphere. To the left of the living quarters was a small bathroom tent, with a canvas hip-bath hanging on a nearby tree. Twelve respectable looking brown hens scraped and foraged around among the cut reeds and in the earth close by, perpetually harassed by one of the dogs, which insisted on taking over any comfortable looking dust bath which a hen had made for herself.

John organised my luggage and was then introduced to the Kays' boss boy, Kisi, who took him away to show him his quarters. Then Robert turned to me. 'I expect you're dying to see Chinky and Timmy,' he said, and took me off to see their two pet lions.

Timmy was tied to a tree by a long chain. He was a dwarf lion which they had reared from a cub, having taken pity on him and bought him when they first met him in a circus that visited Bulawayo. When he stood up, his short front legs suggested a bow-legged and plump bishop in tight gaiters. From this first moment my relationship with him was uneasy. There was obvious friendliness in his eyes when he played with Robert or June, but he had no affection to spare for me: he tended, rather, to fasten aggressively on to my ankles.

It was very different with Chinky. I fell for her at once, and I felt that the sentiment was reciprocated. She was housed in the back of an old vehicle, since the chief men of the local Batawana tribe had insisted that she should be caged when in their vicinity. She was the largest lioness I had ever seen, and, although she was two and a half years old, she still carried on her flanks some trace of the spot-markings of cubhood. Her hazel-coloured eyes were large but somewhat slit-like, somewhat oriental: her muzzle was fawn, and her chin was forcefully shaped and snowy white. Part of the side of the truck had been cut away for cleaning purposes, and she would reach her paws out through this narrow slot to play, patting at one's hand or arm as a kitten pats at a reel of cotton, with her claws always retracted. When I went inside to make her closer acquaintance she licked first my hand, then my arm, then my cheek: her tongue was as rough as the surface of a pineapple, but our friendship was now sealed.

Robert cooked a superb curry, and after dinner we talked. He and June, I learned, had fallen in love with the natural beauty of these swamp-lands and had dedicated themselves to the protection of the unspoilt wildlife of this isolated inland delta. Robert had served in the British Army, then in the Palestine Police, then – during World War II – in the Royal Air Force, being stationed in Southern Rhodesia: here in the swamps with June he was wonderfully contented and cheerful, subject only to fits of irritation when the subject of conversation turned to the ways of modern youth. June was artistic, vivacious and petite: whenever possible, even in the heat of the day, she would sit down to her typewriter and work steadily away – at some further article on game conservation in N'gamiland, perhaps, or at another chapter of her second book, *Wild Eden*.

It was certainly a lovely and Eden-like place. We sat and talked in the dusk under the canvas of the verandah: through a gap in the trees we could see before us, until the light failed, a wide panorama of river and swamp-land. The hens roosted in the safe trees of the camp, and the dogs sprawled asleep on the rug by the tent door – all but one of them, Gilly-Anne, who had decided to be my favourite animal against all competition and therefore kept her head pressed against my legs and her eyes fixed sentimentally upon mine.

A peaceful moment – until Robert dropped his bombshell. Casually, as though asking for a glass of water, he said: 'When you go back to Jersey, would you take Chinky with you?'

'Take Chinky?' I gasped in amazement; and then, playing for time and frightened of commitment, I stammered: 'Wh – *what in*?'

'Oh, I've thought of that. I've arranged for a firm in Bulawayo to make a travelling-cage for her, and Riley's Transport ought to be bringing it here before the month is out.'

'Yes, but ... but why?'

'Well, a fortnight ago the authorities here told us that we had to have Chinky taken out of N'gamiland. We couldn't go with her: we've made this place our home. So we were at our wits' end; but then June had the brilliant idea of cabling your zoo. They said that they would be delighted to have her, provided that you were willing to travel with her. And I knew there wouldn't be any question about that ... '

I recognised the hand of fate: I was stuck with a lioness as travelling-companion. And when I came to think of it, I decided that if I was to have one animal, I might as well have a collection. Robert and June were very willing to help, and it was decided that when the travelling-cage had arrived and when I had received the permissions that were needed if I was to collect animals, we would move camp to the Kwaai or Machaba River in the northern regions of the swamps, where there should be any amount of game to see and capture.

Things were taking shape. The Kays were very much relieved to have Chinky's future settled; I had made a good start on what I hoped would prove an affectionate and sympathetic relationship with her; there was interesting work ahead; meanwhile, I was very nicely accommodated in the DUKW – more comfortably, I reflected, than the soldiers were accommodated when this same amphibious vehicle took them to the Normandy beaches. So I fell asleep in high satisfaction.

N'gamiland was then a native reserve area administered by the Colonial Office. Geographically it is like a large inland delta, with waters flowing from the Angola highlands in the north, through the Caprivi strip, and then spreading out into the Okavango swamps; these drain into the shallow lake of N'gami, then peter out into the northern Kalahari in Lake Dow and the M'kuri-M'kuri salt flats.

The swamps were very isolated since the nearest railhead was some three hundred miles away across arid desert, with few good roads and poor communications generally. Moreover, most of the area was occupied by the tsetse fly. For these reasons, the wildlife was pretty well intact. But now it was in danger. Because of the political upheavals in East Africa the big safari firms were looking elsewhere for places where they could bring their rich clients; they had their eye on the Okavango, and were sending representatives to survey the prospects.

This commercialism could do a lot of damage, and the Kays saw it as a challenge: they wanted to get at least some part of the swamp-land recognised as a non-hunting area, and they also wanted to set up a N'gamiland Fauna Preservation Society, an official body with teeth that could be in operation before the safari firms could move in. I was very much in sympathy with them; for my part, I wanted to see as much as possible of the wildlife of the region, and this would help them indirectly, since when I returned to England I would be able to report to influential bodies such as the World Wildlife Fund and the Fauna Preservation Society. Meanwhile, I looked forward to seeing the concentrations of wildlife in the Okavango; my only anxiety was that this purpose might be hampered if I burdened myself with too large a collection too quickly.

Before I could start collecting there were a great many regulations which needed to be complied with. But first of all I had to ask and receive the permission of Mahumahati Moremi, Queen Regent of the Batawana: this was a native reserve area, within which no European could own property and within which the Africans had the last say in all matters.

This meant a formal call. The Queen Regent lived in a pair of whitewashed buildings, which were somewhat out of place – rather suburban – among the more natural-looking mud huts that surrounded them. Robin dressed for the occasion, immaculate in white shirt, white shorts, and white stockings: the best I could muster was a clean bush-jacket, which was perhaps suitable for my role as a keen naturalist. I had never met a Queen Regent before, and I approached in some nervousness, feeling rather like an ambassador about to present his credentials.

Mahumahati Moremi turned out to be a small plump lady, dressed in European style. She was sitting behind a desk when we came in: Robin started to tell her what I wanted to do, emphasising that my chief motive was conservation, and she listened attentively, as did two tall Africans who stood behind her. All three looked at me with obvious interest, and I felt embarrassed: it is difficult to know what to do when three people are looking you up and down while another speaks on your behalf. What was the correct protocol? Should I smile at them? Should I try to look like a keen high-powered scientist whom they ought to respect, or like a vague naturalist whom they could safely indulge? I decided that until I received the Queen Regent's permission, a look of serious anxiety would be the best thing.

After an endless five minutes of uncertainty she agreed to my request, but (I gathered) without entirely believing my story: she seemed to suspect that what I really wanted to do was to collect some wild animals and breed them for meat, as with domestic livestock. Before we went, one of the two Africans in attendance told me that I would have to pay a nominal fee to the tribal treasury, as their law stipulated that a fee should be paid whenever animals were exported from N'gamiland: he therefore wanted to see the collection before it left the country so that he could assess the amount of tax that would be due. This struck me as instant law-making: I knew perfectly well that the question had never arisen before, since I was the first person to collect live specimens in this part of Africa. But I had no intention of disputing the point, and I bowed, shook the graciously extended royal hand, and thanked the Queen wholeheartedly for her co-operation. To mark our gratitude Robert gave her two guinea fowls which he had shot that morning.

My next step was to go and see the District Commissioner, and get the blessing of the European administration and a typed permit. The DC seemed pleased to see a new face: he told me that he had been at school with Peter Scott and was naturally interested in wildfowl and in all kinds of wildlife. He proved to be extremely helpful, and passed me on to the Veterinary Department. Here I was given permission to move animals within the boundaries of N'gamiland, but not to export them to Francistown: that would need separate authorisation when the time came.

As I left the administrative centre the DC came running after me to say that there was one bird which he did *not* authorise me to take away, namely, a fish eagle which was in the habit of perching on a dead tree opposite his house. This bird has the distinctive habit of throwing back its head and uttering a clear six-bar call which is one of the finest sounds of Africa: the DC didn't want to lose his own local performer.

I managed to buy a number of old wooden boxes and two rolls of wire netting from a local trading store: I took these back to camp, and started John on the task of dismantling the boxes and rebuilding them as general-purpose cages. We also made a number of wooden frames, covered with wire netting, which could be lined with hessian and fixed together to serve as cages for any larger birds that I might secure. I was working in the dark, of course, since I had no idea of what species I might capture, or in what quantity: the only thing I could do was to make several cages of different sizes and supplement these when required. I also ordered half a dozen reed baskets to be made, of a type that I had seen locally, but to my specification: these would also make good cages for birds or – if I caught no birds – good presents when I came home.

By extreme good fortune a young pair of black spur-winged geese came into my possession, constituting – together with Chinky – the first members of my N'gamiland collection. A man called Dave Calver, who lived at Maun, had bought them from an African and intended to fatten them up for food: when I heard of this, through Robert, I drove into Maun at once and offered to buy them, if he would keep them for another six weeks at my expense. Fortunately he agreed, and took me behind the house to see them. The spur-winged goose is an odd-looking creature, especially at this early stage of its life. The plumage of these two was just changing to a greenish-black on the back and the neck; they were white underneath, and their beaks and legs were pinkish-red. I went to pick up the young gander, and he tried to strike at me with his right wing: I clearly saw the carpal spur from which this species is named, and I could well imagine how painfully effective this would be if one were attacked by an adult specimen.

Next came a very welcome invitation. A coloured man and five Africans, all connected with the local administration, were planning a weekend in the Chuchubegha region, some forty-five miles to the west of Maun; and they suggested that

June and Robert and I might like to come along with them. We would see a big concentration of game, including buffalo. This invitation was not entirely disinterested: the Batawana tribe were in the habit of shooting for the pot, with no close season, and if this weekend party succeeded in shooting a buffalo, they would be glad of a second vehicle to help bring the meat back.

June knew how much I would value the experience, and she nobly volunteered to stay behind and look after the animals. John and I set forth with the party. It was rather a featureless journey: the track to Chuchubegha looked like any other sandy track, and the mopane bushes looked like any other mopane bushes. The destructive grazing of goats was much in evidence during the first fifteen to twenty miles of our journey. At one point a goat jumped out and ran along in front of us, sticking to the centre of the track in its panic, slowing us down considerably, refusing to turn aside even though Robert kept his hand on the horn. Eventually it tripped and stumbled angrily off to one side.

Along that track we drove, sometimes over hard-packed sand and sometimes through soft drifts which needed to be taken at speed, until we reached another tsetse-fly control-post. We were not expected and there was nobody on duty: we blew the horn but nobody came. So we drove on. By now there was no definable track, and the driver of the leading vehicle had to thread his way through the light bush, between small copses and thickets, across tracts of parched yellow grassland, then through the mopane once more, and so onwards, with the spoor of both vehicles stretching behind.

We came to a small graceful herd of impala. They stopped grazing as the trucks approached, and the nearest buck sniffed the air, trying to catch our scent. Then, to my amazement, the sound of a rifle shot came from the Africans' truck in front: I actually heard the smack of the bullet as it tore into flesh, and saw the buck stagger sideways from the force of the impact, then pull himself together and run, some way behind his harem of five or six does. The leading truck drove straight on, making no attempt to follow up the wounded animal: left to itself it was certain to die a slow and painful death. So Robert swung aside, drove in search, located the buck within five minutes, and put it out of its misery. Then the other truck retraced its tracks to find us and perhaps to share in the kill; and Robert had some very pointed remarks to make to the trigger-happy African who had fired that casual and pointless shot. It is one thing to shoot for the pot: this is inevitable, in fact, in regions where the tsetse fly prevents any keeping of domestic animals and makes protein food hard to come by. But it is quite another thing to use small game for casual target practice; and Robert told the guilty man exactly what he thought of him.

The episode left a nasty taste in our mouths, but we were consoled by the spectacular and rewarding drive during the next hour. Three reticulated giraffes towered above the long grass, browsing from the tops of stunted trees until they saw the trucks, then cantering away in their ungainly fashion; eight warthogs, disturbed from wallowing in some damp cotton-soil, ran in disorder for the nearest cover; a herd of the shaggy tsessabe, some twelve in number, crashed through the high reeds by a small stream. Their white-ringed behinds made ideal targets as they vanished, but nobody was going to risk Robert's anger for a second time that afternoon.

Around every corner, it seemed, we would come across zebra, or wildebeest (brindled gnu), and each one would snort and swish its tail in indignation at our noise and intrusion. The coloured man in the leading truck, Benjamin by name, stopped to tell Robert that he had orders to shoot one wildebeest as well as a buffalo; and then, within moments, we heard another shot and saw a wildebeest stumbling helplessly to the ground. I felt a desperate desire to intervene and defend and save it, though of course it was too late: I still thought in terms of innocent life and the brutality of sudden killing, and I could not come to terms with the economic necessity of such behaviour. And it was such a noble beast, suggesting a heraldic unicorn to me, though without the frontal horn. Benjamin chopped off its tail and threw it to me as a souvenir; I accepted it reluctantly, and I still possess it, the relic of an undeserved martyrdom.

Benjamin and his Batawana friends now set about carving the animal up like professional butchers, loading the legs and the other best cuts on to their trucks. Then we moved on, leaving most of the carcase behind for the carrion lovers, the marabou storks and the vultures. They had started to gather round as soon as the shot was fired – almost before the animal hit the ground – and the marabous had prodded the ground with impatience while the butchery went on, while the vultures perched on the trees around, hunched up, looking really devilish with their hooked beaks and their evil glittering eyes. As soon as we moved away they all closed in, and we left them to it, as they tore at the steaming flesh and quarrelled and pushed to get at the choicest morsels.

We drove on, with Henry – the male cocker spaniel – lying sprawled across my lap with his head out of the window, ecstatically inhaling the odour of fresh meat from the truck in front. Robert had brought him along to get him used to life without his mate, Gilly-Anne, and he obviously thought that there was a feast in store that would amply compensate him for this temporary divorce. He was right. Benjamin halted his truck by a small copse, flanked on the west by a stream and surrounded on the other sides by grassland, and here we pitched camp, lit a fire, and arranged our camp beds. The meal was a simple one – boiled rice with grilled wildebeeste steak – and the surroundings were not those of a luxurious restaurant; but the most fastidious gourmet would have found that meat succulent beyond compare, and all of us, eight men and one dog, retired for the night in the contentment of repletion.

The night was cloudless, and as I lay on my camp-bed and looked up into the huge African night, with the sounds of the bush all round me, I felt a wonderful sense of universal peace. One of the Africans nursed the fire, keeping up a good blaze throughout the night: Henry lay in the shadows, sleeping off his banquet of wildebeest. Every so often the high-pitched cry of a leopard would be heard, and Henry would take little notice, merely blinking in its direction. It was the same when we heard the roaring of two lions somewhere upwind of us. But when we heard the short cackle of a hyena, Henry sprang up and barked and then seemed to regret it, looking at us for reassurance, and sitting down vigilantly between our beds and the fire. It is not always wise (he was thinking) to betray one's presence to a possible predator.

We had breakfasted and struck camp by seven next morning, and I learned with mixed feelings that the buffalo shooting came next. Well, at least we were going to feed the Batawana: it was not a case of rich men looking for trophies, or business men exporting the animal wealth of N'gamiland for profit. And, as things turned out, the next few hours were among the most exciting of my life.

We spotted a herd of buffalo in a small clearing, but they moved off before a shot could be fired, into vegetation too thick and dense for the truck to follow. So we went after them on foot, Benjamin leading, his .375 rifle carried at the trail. For some five minutes we pressed on through the trees and bushes: my heavy binoculars kept getting caught on branches or banging against my chest, so that I had to carry them. I could see nothing whatever of the signs our guide was following: I felt bothered and lost.

Then Benjamin stopped and studied some hoof-marks. They were plainly those of a buffalo, but how old were they? He considered the question, moved off experimentally down two alternative trails, came back, and beckoned us to follow. On we moved, speaking only in whispers, and after about half an hour we found confirmation that we were on the right track – buffalo manure, and so fresh that the animals must be close at hand.

As we moved cautiously through the dense vegetation, aware that a clumsy step on a twig or a rotten branch would put the game to flight, I felt that this was the real art and craft of the hunter – a very different thing from the easy slaughter, so cheaply done in open country with telescopic rifles, which is flatteringly called 'big-game hunting'.

Now we came upon some manure that was still steaming, and the horsey smell of buffalo was all about us. The herd was upwind: they might hear us but would not smell us as we approached. Benjamin held up a hand and we stopped in our tracks: then he advanced in total silence and crouched down beneath a low-hanging branch. We waited tensely.

The silence shattered: we heard the bang of his rifle and then the fleshy smack of a hit, and at once the herd was snorting and thundering through the undergrowth in our direction, emerging from cover, seeing us, then swerving away at the last minute. The wounded beast had apparently remained behind and was hiding somewhere.

We were now in a tense situation. The African buffalo is considered by some big-game hunters to be the most danger-ous of all African game to go after: he is extremely cunning when wounded, and can survive many bullets. We heard a distant crackling from the vanishing herd, but in front of us there was an ominous silence. Robert unslung the rifle he had brought along for self-protection, and we watched as Benjamin crept forward with every sense alert. He must have been almost upon the wounded buffalo when it broke cover and came charging at him with head lowered. The coolness of his nerve was amazing: unhurriedly, he dropped to one knee and fired. The buffalo hit the ground like a ton of rocks, shot through the heart: a few feet further, and he would have killed his killer.

I congratulated Benjamin warmly, and was rather surprised to find myself doing so: I am not normally enthusiastic about the deaths of animals. But in this case the odds were about as even as they could possibly be, and one could not fail to admire the tracker's skill and the marksman's composure at a moment of extreme danger.

We left the two Africans by the carcase, and went back by a shorter route to the trucks. Henry greeted us in high

Going home: (*above left*) Chinky looking apprehensive; (*above right*) how we packed them in; (*below*) full house.

Ostrich from N'Gamiland – 'D'you know you're taller than me?'

hysteria: he had been safely shut up in the cab in Robert's truck, but had obviously felt terrified at being alone in such wild country. Then we drove back and helped with the butchering of the steaming carcase, cutting branches and loading the meat upon them, and so dragging it to the trucks, which were soon filled almost to capacity. Africa's varied sanitary squad, from vultures to dung beetles, started to gather in readiness for the tidying-up operation.

Henry was in a great state of alarm, and would not even sample the meat: he refused to get back into the cab until it became clear that we were coming too. (He was only a brave dog when Gilly-Anne was around to be impressed.) But eventually we were loaded up and started off for Maun, stopping at various African villages on the way to distribute shares of the meat, which was very much welcomed.

And so we arrived back home at the base camp, and feasted upon the strongly flavoured buffalo meat: there were large bones for the lions and the dogs had their share too, though Henry was still off his food and feeling very sorry for himself after the terrible experience of being alone in the truck. The only thing wrong with the meat was that there was so much of it: we seemed to live on nothing else for the next week, with buffalo liver or kidneys for breakfast, buffalo steak for lunch, and buffalo curry in the evening. It was rather like those occasions when you prepare a mountain of food for a party but none of it gets eaten, so that you have to work your way through it for days afterwards.

I now intended to explore the region more thoroughly. But first, I had to recover from an unpleasant encounter with some maggot flies. I had washed one of my shirts and spread it out to dry in the sun, and the flies must then have laid their eggs in it: when I put it back on, the eggs had hatched, and the larvae dug their way into my back, causing the most awful irritation, which got worse as they dug deeper. June came to my rescue: I sat on a stool and bent forward, and she smothered the entry tunnels with Germolene. This meant that they had to break surface in order to breathe, and could

G

then be plucked forth: after a few days of this treatment I was free of them, and could start my explorations.

I used a small aluminium dinghy with an outboard motor: Robert kept it as a tender for the DUKW, and on this suitable craft I cruised around the swampy and watery regions of the Thamalakane. The bird life was entrancing. There were pied kingfishers everywhere, hovering in the air, perfectly still, then diving upon their prey with remarkable speed and accuracy. There were brightly coloured pygmy geese – the drakes with breasts and flanks of chestnut, bills of bright orange, and heads adorned with arresting green patches on either side. There were African jacanas or lily-trotters, picking their way over the plate-like leaves of the water lilies with huge feet that were perfectly adapted to that medium of travel. Above me, in the branches of dead trees, frequently I saw a white-breasted cormorant: he would perch up there and survey the clear waters, and then dive down to pick up a fish in his long beak. High above the water, I would often see also the majestic white front of the fish eagle.

I could well understand how Robert and June, having intended to travel the length of Africa from south to north, should have stopped on the way and settled down in this Okavango paradise.

Back at the camp, I found bad news: poor Timmy was badly constipated. This was a problem I had not met before but might very well meet again, so I took careful note of the treatment and the patient's progress. First of all we tried the simple device of pouring human-type laxatives liberally on to his food. He wouldn't touch it: there was nothing for it, we decided, but an enema, and we borrowed an enema set from the small hospital at Maun.

It is not as easy as you might think to give a male lion an enema. For one thing Timmy disliked having his hind-quarters touched: in fact, being off-colour, he preferred to be left entirely alone. We tried blandishments, with Robert tickling Timmy's chin and stroking his neck, while June stood by with the enema tube at the ready and I held the bottle of soapy water. But Timmy wasn't to be fooled: he became rather angry, and demanded to be left alone.

It was plainly a case for anaesthesia. We mixed seven and a half grains of nembutal with some milk, and managed to pour it down his throat: then, for the next two hours, we stood around and waited for him to turn drowsy. But he didn't, and we began to be seriously worried: he might have an intestinal obstruction, which could only be resolved by surgery. He hadn't had anything to eat for four days.

So Robert went back to the hospital and managed to charm some chloroform out of the people there: two of them came along to help. The method used was crude but effective: we took a sack, and put at the bottom of it a good-sized wad of cottonwool, freely soaked with chloroform, and then Robert closed in and dragged the sack over Timmy's head, while the rest of us secured his legs. June held the enema tube, John held the bottle; Robert kept the cottonwool over Timmy's nose until he felt him relax. Then, triumphantly, June managed to get some olive oil and several pints of soapy water successfully into him; and we left poor outraged Timmy alone so that nature could take its course. He looked much better the next day, and ate some minced steak: we followed up the treatment with a couple of intra-muscular shots of terramycin, and soon it became obvious that the constipation was lavishly cured.

So far I had not started any serious collecting in this region. But I couldn't help leaving a baited wire trap at the back of the camp, just to see what happened. At first I made the mistake of putting it too near the camp, and thus caught several of Robert's brown hens, to their extreme indignation. When I put it further away, I caught a most endearing little rodent, the bulbous-eyed Bechuanaland gerbil: the first mammal of this collection, and I took it happily back to the camp and lodged it in a spacious wooden box.

As I moved around our encampment I could never pass Chinky without stopping to have a word with her. When I approached she would stand up and look at me appealingly, then lower her snow-white chin and utter a gently welcoming 'wow': she was irresistible.

One of my tasks was cleaning out her home in the Dodge truck: I would run it down to the riverside, and then use a long hoe to scrape out the soiled reeds and her water dish. She took all this to be a game, and made things much harder by patting incessantly at the hoe with her large paws, and also by whisking her water dish back to the farthest corner of the truck just when I had managed to coax it within my reach. But I always won in the end; I would swill down the inside of the truck with buckets of water from the river, clean and refill the water dish, and then poke in a new floor-covering of the fresh reeds which John had already cut for me.

It was now time to prepare for our journey up to the northern regions of the swamps, and Robert decided to give the engine of the DUKW a thorough testing. It was an amphibious vehicle or craft, with six-wheel drive and with no fewer than ten forward as well as four reverse gears. I tried the controls: I felt unconquerable, as though I was driving an immense tank. Then Robert took it into the river, and tried out its aquatic capabilities by a short trip downstream and up again: every so often the wheels would touch bottom and it would function momentarily as a land vehicle instead of a boat. A versatile craft: it served as our power-station as well as our transport, since Robert had installed a small generator on board, which – if run for an hour each morning – would charge the batteries so as to give us all the current we needed in the evening. But it was a noisy hour, and if one desired to talk without bellowing, one needed to be away from camp while the generator was running.

All was now ready for our northerly expedition: I could hardly wait to start, the collector's itch being powerfully on me. Restlessly I looked around at the camp vicinity. Every day I had seen squirrels in the fig trees above and heard their click-click noises, and I knew that they were in the habit of making early-morning raids on our food-store. So I got to work on the spot, strapping the smaller of my two wire traps on to a broad branch that was much in use as a squirrels' highway. It was Henry who drew my attention to the result: there he was next morning, sitting below and barking, appearing to think that he had effected the capture. I took the cage down and opened it, and found inside a small green tree squirrel which – from the black speckles on its back – I could identify as a specimen of *Peraxerus cepapi maunensis*. It seemed too bulky a name for so small an animal, and since the textbook gave it no English name, I decided that it was to be simply a Maun squirrel. It was quite exceptionally nervous and seemed likely to damage its head against the walls of the trap; so I decided to release it, and to catch further specimens in the same way at a later date, so that they could live in a padded box and have only a short time of captivity and travel.

John had made a supply of collapsible cages and wire frames, somewhat oddly proportioned but capable of being erected quickly; my bird baskets had also come, and I had paid a ridiculously low price for them; my permits were all in order.

And so I embarked upon this second stage of my collection, feeling slightly more confident now, more plausibly a real trapper of real animals, by reason of my first experience in Rhodesia.

CHAPTER 6

Flamingoes, Wattled Cranes and Aardvarks

NOW, as we were ready to set forth, another difficulty arose. Chinky's travelling-cage had not arrived from Bulawayo. I did not need it immediately; on the other hand, I did not want to set out for the northern swamps until I was completely sure that it would be there at Maun when I came back, so that Chinky could be transferred to it at once, and embark upon the journey back to the Channel Islands with the rest of the collection that I hoped to gather. At that stage, with a possibly large number of animals cramped into travelling-cages, delay would be most undesirable.

In order to keep us usefully occupied while we waited for the cage, Robert suggested that we should go for a week to Lake N'gami to see the large collection of birds that abounded there, and perhaps to net some. June was busy writing yet another article for the South African press – a condemnation of the growing trade in cheetah, leopard, and serval skins – and she was rather glad to have us out of the way, so that she could enjoy the peace and quiet that every writer needs. Robert and I took with us Kisi the cook boy and John, and we loaded the truck with some baskets and cage-frames, plus a week's supply of food. Henry also came along with us: he jumped into the cab under the impression that we were only driving into Maun to collect the lions' meat, and we decided not to make an issue of it.

Our drive took us forty-eight miles to the south-west, to the small trading post of Sehitwa. The track ran, at one point, through a forest of ghost trees; they had been drowned by severe flooding two years before, and there was not a scrap of greenery upon any of them. They looked like something found on a lunar landscape, bare and dead: it was hard to see them as trees, hard also to imagine floods in a district that was now so parched and arid.

We drove on, and encountered a family of ostrich. When they saw the truck they split up; the brownish hen bird made off with her brood of five chicks, while the black-bodied male walked slowly away in the opposite direction, feigning injury and spreading his wings, gallantly trying to draw away from his family, and upon himself, any danger that there might be. Robert noticed that one of the chicks had parted from its mother and was stumbling back along the track towards us, unseen by either parent; so he stopped the truck and got out, taking care not to be seen by the devoted father, and through the driver's mirror I then saw him run back along the track and perform a kind of rugger tackle upon the chick, securing it and then gently gathering it up. He brought it into the cab, and we started off again; but after twenty yards the truck stopped without warning. At the same moment the ostrich chick, which was on my lap, relieved itself lavishly and liquidly all over my trousers.

We responded to this twofold crisis like true Englishmen. In a moment Robert had the bonnet open and was tinkering with the engine, while I emerged from the cab, shook myself clean as far as this was possible, and set about helping him. The father ostrich had apparently lost interest and had made off to join his family; thus, to leave my hands free, I tied a piece of raffia to the chick's left leg and tethered him to a nearby mopane. (My bird baskets were inconveniently hard to get at in emergency: they were packed under our week's supply of provisions.) So I got to work alongside Robert, and was soon covered in diesel oil, and found myself wondering whether mechanical work was dirtier than animal work; but then, all at once, back came the angry father ostrich. We hastily took refuge in the cab, and Henry looked up at us in mild surprise, having no idea of the great events that were taking place outside: we looked out in amazement as the father ostrich carefully pecked away at the raffia until his chick was free. It was pleasant to see them reunited: I wanted to have a pair of ostrich, but this one was not destined for my collection.

At Sehitwa we visited a small store owned by a Greek trader who lived with an African wife and a retinue of chocolate coloured children. When he learned that I had come to N'gamiland to collect animals he asked me to follow him round to the back of the store and there showed me an ostrich and an impala too, both of them living in his hen-run. 'They are yours for ten rand each,' he said, rather implying that I was certain to buy whatever he offered. I told him that I wouldn't be able to take the impala, but would be interested in the ostrich if he could hold on to it for me for another six weeks. She was a fine bird, almost four feet high, and when I looked her over appraisingly she simpered bashfully, like a young beauty in the slave market. Her pale neck was striped with delicate broken lines in pastel shades, her large eyes were overshadowed by long flirtatious lashes, and her flightless wings sat on her body like powder puffs on either side. The Greek had been keeping her for five months. At night it was her custom to join the impala and the hens under a thatched lean-to, and the hens would roost all over her body as she crouched down, possibly taking her for one of themselves. The warmth so provided had saved her life. In the natural state ostrich chicks take refuge under their mother's wings, and so maintain a daytime temperature in the cold night: they cannot survive without such help.

This part of N'gamiland had little or no tsetse fly, and it was the major cattle-rearing area of the region. Most of the Africans were of the Damara tribe, which had fled from German South-West Africa at the beginning of the century: they were subject to the indigenous Batawana, though the latter were fewer in number and poorer in cattle.

As we drove on to Lake N'gami, twelve miles to the south,

we could see that we were indeed in cow country. Four Africans passed us on the track and waved cheerfully; they were wearing cowboy-type hats and riding fine horses, and they were engaged in herding some three hundred head of beef cattle away from the lake to spend the night in some vast kraal or corrall. Behind the herd a great cloud of dust arose, making it hard for Robert to see where we were going and to avoid the many obstacles. But eventually we emerged from the dust and the scrub-trees and into open flat country like a steppe: then, like a mirage, the lake itself appeared on the horizon. We were surrounded, as we came closer, by an increasingly deafening tumult of abundant bird life.

The sun was sinking fast, and we stopped to set up camp for the night, lighting a fire and setting up our camp-beds in the open. John and Kisi preferred to sleep in the back of the truck. Then, as always during our stay by the shores of Lake N'gami, we were privileged to see a sunset of the most breathtaking kind. The whole horizon became a vast red-hot furnace, into which the sun sank like a fireball. Thereafter the night became cool, which we found refreshing after the hot motoring of the day. We dined agreeably off steak and rice with some rather warm canned beer, and then, with Henry lying between our camp-beds, we soon fell asleep under a ceiling of radiant stars.

Lake N'gami covers an area of some forty-five square miles. It was discovered by Livingstone in the mid-nineteenth century, and possesses in all probability one of the richest concentrations of bird life to be found anywhere in the world. There are even pelicans: in Livingstone's time they used the lake as a breeding place, but now – owing to the encroachments of domestic cattle – they merely congregate there. Most of the lake is only a few feet deep; it is rich in plankton, and has a matted forest of oxygen-producing plants growing from its muddy bottom. It is because of these water plants, and also because of the saltiness of the water that comes from evaporation, that the place is attractive to so many kinds of bird.

Next morning we drove along by the lakeside, going as close to the edge as the firmness of the ground would permit. We passed groups of marabou storks which would preen beneath their wings, then shake their shaggy necks, then return to their endless preening. The small sacred ibis, black of neck and head, would prod around in the weeds, looking for insect delicacies: the African avocet too, with its upturned beak. Ducks, terns and plovers flew busily here and there: some large wood ibis bunched together about two hundred yards from the shore, standing as though on red stilts in order to keep their plumage dry. In the distance, near the middle of the lake, we saw the pastel shades of the greater and lesser flamingo; also those pelicans, ill-proportioned birds perhaps, with their outsize beaks and bloated throats. And all these different birds kept up their varied and continual cries, unremittingly.

We continued our drive along the east bank of the lake, with the sun's heat battering down upon every inch of the wide country. On the southern shore we chose a dry grassy stretch of ground for our base and stopped there. We needed shade badly, and so we fixed a big piece of canvas by two corners to the top of the truck, and supported the other two corners on poles which we sank into the ground: under this canopy we could sit in some comfort. Then we offloaded our provisions and my own equipment: baskets chiefly to serve as bird cages, and also four aluminium rods which could be fixed together to make a pair of twelve-foot poles. These had been specially made for me according to the specification of Reay Smithers in Salisbury, who knew Bechuanaland well and the conditions there: the idea was that I would be able to hang my almost invisible and therefore bird-catching mist-nets between them in any sort of country, without relying upon trees.

We lunched off some refreshing water melons which we had bought from the Greek trader; then, wearing only shorts and bush hats, we started to wade into the lake and among waterweeds that tickled our legs. John carried the two aluminium poles, no doubt wondering what I was going to do with them. Henry took a couple of steps into the lake, just far enough in to get muddy, and then returned to dry land and started to bark a loud protest. Robert spoke to him rather sharply: he was disturbing the birds. So Henry went back to the truck feeling misunderstood and martyred; we discovered later that he had jumped on to his master's camp-bed to sleep there, covering it with the lake mud that had clung to his person.

We did not go very far into the lake. When using a mist-net of this sort, one of the great rules is that you must always stay nearby, so that a netted specimen does not have too much time to entangle itself and thus get hurt, as well as damaging the net. We would be able to see the net easily enough, and to see when it had caught a bird, wherever it was; but we would not be able to move quickly through those weedy shallows, so the net had to be close at hand. We dug the sharpened end of one of the rods into the mud, and then, before attaching the other half, I took a brand-new mist-net out of its plastic package and attached it to the top of the pole, then hoisted it into position. Some thirty feet away we erected the other pole in the same way, taking care not to get the mist-net wet. The top of the net now stood some 9ft above the water; and there were four tension cords running through the $1\frac{1}{2}$in mesh, thus forming three shelf-like pockets, within which any bird that flew into the net would be caught. (Without such an arrangement, it would simply bounce off the net and continue its flight.)

Now we had to trust to luck. For one thing, if a flamingo or a wood ibis flew into the net, it would be the net that suffered, and disastrously. Then, how could we know that any birds would happen to fly in the right direction? I had read how ornithologists use these nets when working along some small stream or river: they stretch the net across, from one side to the other, and since the birds commonly fly up and down the river, their chances of catching them are good. But the open surface of a large lake is a different matter. We had to place our trust in the near-invisibility of the net, and hope that some of the smaller water fowl would happen to fly between the poles: with luck, a scared ibis or two.

So we waded back to the shore and to that very welcome shade. I sat on my camp-bed and watched the bird life through my binoculars: I felt like a football fan, waiting passionately for the moment when the ball would come flying between the posts and into the net. But as there was nobody trying to kick the ball through, I felt that my chances were more like those of the people who go in for football pools.

Then about an hour after we came back from the lake I saw something bulging and struggling in one of the pockets on the net. I shot up from the camp-bed and bounded into the lake, stumbling in my excitement and getting my shorts covered with mud and weeds, startling Henry into a frenzy of barking. When I reached the net and identified the bird that was struggling into a deeper and deeper entanglement, I saw in some disappointment that it was an avocet – not a species I wanted. I had a fearful task to get it loose without damaging the net. A bird in this situation will get the thin nylon twisted round its neck, over its wings, round and between its legs, and as you free one part, another becomes further entangled. In the end I had to enlist both Robert and John to hold each part of the avocet securely as it was dis-entangled in its turn, thus preventing re-entanglement. And so we got it free.

The net survived this adventure; and later on in the day, it survived a heavier threat. We were just going to take it down for the night, when I was appalled to see a number of assorted cattle wading in the lake in its direction. They were between me and the net: if I ran out, I would drive them into it. I considered a flanking movement, but this was out of the question. I had to trust to luck. Apparently the African cowboys whom we had met before had chosen this stretch of water for the watering of their cattle in order to gratify their own curiosity about our presence and purposes by the lakeside. I crossed my fingers and held my breath while the cattle splashed along by my precious net, and in the end no harm was done, though one of the beasts did stumble against one of the guy-ropes that supported the nearer pole.

Our next concern was with the flamingoes and pelicans. These larger birds tended to stick to the middle of the lake, and it took us a good forty-five minutes of wading to get within reasonable distance of them; as we drew nearer we had to shout louder and louder if we wanted to communicate, so deafening was their clamour.

The pelicans were the most suspicious; they would launch themselves into the air if we came anywhere near them, flying off then to the northern part of the lake. The flamingoes were more trusting: when we came within eighty or a hundred yards of them they would start to move away, in groups of about twenty, but only taking to the air if we closed in on them too quickly.

They used to take a regular evening flight, all together, and it was wonderful to behold. Just before sunset they would take off in one immense flight, with their long necks and crooked black beaks held out before them: their pink bodies would fill the western sky, contrasting beautifully with the fiery shades of the declining sun. Then they would come spiralling gracefully back to alight close to the lakeshore where they would pass the night.

I wanted to capture some, but my first attempt ended in muddy failure. Robert and I decided that we would approach them at night-time; we thought that as they slept – each bird balancing on one leg, with its head tucked under one wing – we would be able to creep up undetected and close in and rugger-tackle them. Clouds would help to darken the night and conceal our advance; a light wind would help also, by carrying our scent away and the noise of our approach too. Unfortunately this particular night was both cloudless and windless.

Slowly we advanced upon the sleeping birds, our bare feet sinking into the soft weeds and mud. We could see the flamingoes plainly before us, some fifteen of them, looking very much like the imitation flamingoes that one can sometimes see in an ornamental pond. But their immobility didn't last. As we approached, one small head came out from under a wing and one small warning noise was uttered, and at once they all started to move off. We were within ten yards of them, and we both thought that swift action was called for, and we leapt forward as one man and dived for the legs of the nearest flamingo. The splash was tremendous; and we emerged hopefully, each hoping to see a bird captive in the other's arms. In fact we saw each other birdless and smothered in slime. We laughed uncontrollably, while the fifteen birds walked away with dignity and unharmed.

The exercise had taught us one thing at least that when approached in this fashion, flamingoes would walk away rather than fly away. This meant that on some later occasion we should be able to drive them into a net.

Next day I reaped a rich harvest from the mist-net, and had my first encounter with the black and white blacksmith plover. This species seemed collectively determined to join my collection, not in ones and twos but in flocks. For the rest of our stay by Lake N'gami they would come streaming into the mist-net, and it would take the three of us – John included – a long time to disentangle them. A painful operation too: their small carpal spurs would prick our hands as they struggled madly against their own liberation. Actually we liberated too many. Two months later, when I was back in England, I was told by John Yealland – the curator of birds at the London Zoo – that he would have been very glad of a few specimens. For us, on the spot, these plovers were just a nuisance; quite apart from the work they made by filling up the net and struggling in its folds, they made other birds suspicious of it, so that they avoided it. We therefore had to keep moving it from one place to another.

In between these onslaughts from the blacksmith plover, I managed to catch two species of teal in the net: the red-billed teal, and the smaller hottentot teal. I was particularly interested in this latter species, as its distribution is confined to this southern half of Africa, and it is not seen as often as the red-billed kind. So I felt that our visit to the lake was beginning to bear fruit, even though John did go through a phase of allowing birds to fly away when I had released them from the net and passed them to him to hold. This was not good for my temper, and once, when he had let a hottentot teal escape. I furiously told him to run after it and catch it. He began to do exactly that, but I called him back. He probably thought I was crazy; but then, the whole of my activities must have seemed rather crazy by African standards.

My baskets now had their first occupants, and I stretched canopies of hessian across their tops, under the lids, so that the birds would not damage themselves by jumping and struggling. I also kept the hessian damp, so that these waterfowl would not dry out and lose the natural oil of their bodies.

By the end of the week the baskets held a small collection: two pairs of the red-billed teal, and three pairs of the hottentot variety. They provided me with a feeding problem. The difficulty was not to know what to give them, since a mixture of corn millet and mealie-meal was certainly right: the difficulty was to get them to eat at all. In captivity they just crouched at the bottom of their baskets and refused to touch anything, regarding themselves as doomed. So I had to coax them, holding the head gently, dabbing the beak into the food. This usually worked. When it failed I had to make little pellets out of the food and work these into the obstinate bird's beak at the side, then close the beak and point it upwards and stroke the neck until the pellet went down.

And so we passed five days by the lakeside, and then took our canopy down and packed up and drove northwards along the western side of the lake. As we went, we saw no fewer than eleven specimens of the majestic wattled crane, foraging along the shore with their mincing dancer-like tread. A tantalising sight: wattled cranes are very seldom seen in zoological parks, and if I could capture a pair, the scope and value of my collection would be wonderfully enhanced. But how *could* I capture them? They are active birds, and in that flat countryside they would be able to see us coming from miles way. I started to dream of a vast net, a mile or so long, to be launched into the air by rockets. . . But then I came down to earth, and remembered that I had just one mist-net, just thirty feet long, holed already by a small duck.

But the frustration became unbearable; I told Robert to stop the truck, and we left John and the cook boy to look after everything and keep the ducks fed, while we went off crane hunting. We stretched out long leg-nooses on the ground, and then we moved slowly around selected cranes, trying to drive them in the right direction. It was a bookies' day, the odds were against us, but we found the suspense exciting. One crane actually did get its feet caught in a noose: our hopes soared but immediately fell, since the bird just danced a little jig and then continued on its way. The sun was merciless, and Robert lost his sun glasses, so that we had to retrace our steps with our eyes on the ground: altogether it was a disappointing day.

We camped a little further on, and decided that before we finally left the lake, we would have another and last shot at flamingo catching. So we used some of the wood and wire frames and made a trap, a big thing like a barn, and fixed this in the lake about half a mile offshore. Then we erected two mist-nets in the shape of a broad V, with the trap at the point: the idea was that we could drive them into the V and thus down into the trap, or at least, into some position where they would be at our mercy.

We waited once again for the cover of night-time, and – but without success – for the further cover of clouds. Then we set forth, stumbling as quietly as possible through the familiar slime and tickle of the lake, alerting the birds but cautiously, not wanting them to panic. It seemed to be working; they started moving off, and in the right direction.

This was getting exciting. Steadily the gap between the

Just back: (*above*) Helen of Troy's Paris – Eared or Lappet-faced vulture; (*below*) Chinky's arrival at Jersey Zoo.

(*above*) Martial Eagle at Jersey Zoo; (*below*) a brace of immature white-headed vultures.

birds and the net work narrowed, and if some flamingo decided to change course, we could easily outflank it and turn it back. We weren't helped by the moonlight and starlight, which showed up the net and the trap with what seemed to us great clarity; but there was no sign that the flamingoes noticed them. On we plodded, sinking and quelching through the weed entangled shallows. We counted eleven specimens, and it seemed that our technique was going to work.

The birds kept up their quiet murmur and their steady progress; but then, as they came within the open jaws of the funnel of net, they suddenly fell into complete disorder and broke ranks noisily. Robert and I reckoned that it was important to force them against the nets, and so we splashed forwards shouting, driving the birds on to those fragile mist-nets and indeed through them. The confusion was frightful: when it was all over Robert and I found ourselves sitting once again on the lake's muddy bottom, alone and birdless.

Next morning, sobered and saddened, we went out to dismantle the trap. There were four blacksmith plovers entrapped in the tattered mist-nets, as though in a last determined effort to join the teal in captivity; and our defeat of the previous night was underlined by the presence there of several pastel-pink feathers. It was obvious that the mist-nets could not be used again: we cut them down from the poles, liberated the plovers, collected the frames, and returned to shore. At least I was learning by experience that some methods of trapping were *not* practical.

So we left Lake N'gami, after a whole week on its shores. I don't think Henry had enjoyed one moment of that week. He didn't like the muddy and weedy waters of the lake; he had continually been shouted at for going too close to the duck-baskets; he had missed Gilly-Anne; his meat ration had been atrocious. Now, as the baskets were loaded up on the back of the truck, it dawned upon him that we were actually going home: he wagged his small copper-coloured tail forgivingly, leapt to his seat in the cab, and sat there bolt upright, his eyes longingly on the north.

H*

At Sehitwa we called again at the Greek's store, and fin-
alised my arrangements for collecting the ostrich. The Greek
came out of the store and peered curiously into the back of the
truck, probably expecting to see any number of flamingoes
and cranes. I had to explain rather sheepishly that these
particular birds had somehow avoided capture, chiefly because
of the time factor: this showed my trapping ability in a
rather poor light, especially in view of the huge quantities
of bird life that crowded there by the lake, begging to be
captured.

We drove back to Maun and on to Robert's base camp on
the Thamalakane, stopping three times on the way so that
I could check up on the teal and keep their baskets damp
and their food topped up. Soon we were home. June, the
lions, the spaniels and the hens all seemed glad to have us
back, and Henry was in heaven. I had a word with Chinky,
and then went to see how my Bechuanaland gerbil was getting
on. I looked into the cage and there it was, sitting in front
of a mound of grain that was nearly as big as itself, and may
have looked much bigger, what with the magnifying curve
of its bulbous eyes. It was applying itself in a dedicated sort
of way to the problem of eating right through this mound of
grain: I decided to make its paradise complete by catching
it a mate.

The next journey that we had in mind would take us up to
the northern region of the swamps, and as two Africans would
stay behind at the base camp, I decided that the teal could
also remain in their care. So John and I set about building an
aviary. We chose a pool by the riverside, with a steady flow
of water to keep it fresh, and we fenced this in, sinking the
wire deeply into the mud for security, and roofing the
enclosure with more wire, supporting this from the con-
venient branch of a fig tree. We scattered reeds over the wire
roof so as to provide shade, and threaded some more reeds
through the bottom part of the wire walls, so as to camouflage
them and discourage the birds from damaging themselves in
fruitless attempts to escape. I put the hottentot teal in first:

they panicked a little, but soon settled down to bathe in the pool. The red-billed teal were also upset at first, but before long the water and the weeds calmed them down and gave them something to do.

We drove into Maun every day to collect provisions for the camp and meat for the lions. On one such trip we saw in front of the truck the long hosepipe shape of a python. Robert asked me if I wanted it. 'Well, yes,' I answered without much enthusiasm, 'I suppose it would be a nice thing to have.' Robert jumped out at once, and with all the agility of a mongoose he grabbed the writhing serpent by the nape of its neck. It was about five feet long, and not at all pleased by this treatment. We hadn't got any kind of box on the truck to put it in, so I hurriedly suggested to Robert that he should hold on to the python while I went back to the camp and fetched one. He took the view that he ought to ride back with us, so he climbed into the cab, python and all. Henry jumped out in terror and refused to come in again: I had to stow him in the back. And so we drove back to camp, with the python winding itself like a creeper around Robert's leg, and darting out its forked tongue in hostility towards everybody and everything.

Back at the camp we disentangled it from Robert and put it in a large box, taking care to keep it out of sight of the gerbil, which would be upset by a meeting. I found that I very much disliked handling this reptile, and I wondered why: after all, I had managed to handle the rock monitor often enough in Rhodesia, and it could have hurt me a good deal more than this python. I decided that this revulsion was a matter of ignorance on my part, and that the snake was probably as nervous of me as I was of him; so inwardly shuddering a little, I set to work on the task of winning his friendship.

My Bechuanaland collection was now beginning to grow and take shape: I had a python, a gerbil, two species of teal, and the prospect of having two spur-winged geese and an ostrich. I also had Chinky, and she was a joy, and would play with me, or with Robert or June, in the most agreeably kittenish manner. John looked upon this phenomenon with never-ending astonishment: for him, a lion was simply a predator, and a danger to be avoided. Even so, he seemed to be taking an interest in this new aspect of the matter, which would be socially useful for him when he returned to his own village at Mazoe. I could see him dining out on this experience for years to come, astounding his cronies with tales of his long fearless involvement with a terrible lioness.

I now heard rumours of another animal, the clawless otter. About a mile upstream from our camp, at the confluence of the small Boro river with the Thamalakane, there were two large posts. I had already seen how these were used by the Batawana tribesmen; they would work their way up to the poles in their dugout canoes, and fix a string gill-net between them, and then go away. When they came back soon afterwards, there would be a few fish in the net. I thought that I could modify this technique and so secure one or two of the clawless otters which (I was now told) abounded thereabouts. Out came my strong nylon animal nets, which had cost me a good deal of money, having been made specially for me at Bridport in Dorset; and I went out during the night in the little aluminum dinghy and fixed these nets between the poles. Then I manoeuvred the dinghy into the cover of a nearby reed bed and settled down to keep watch and see what happened.

It was not an altogether lonely vigil: all around me there was the high-pitched sound of frogs and the french-horn-like belchings of toads. A few mosquitoes alighted on me, but were driven off by my own supremely effective technique of repelling insects, the essence of which is the steady chewing of garlic.

The night moved slowly on: the reeds swayed in the gentle breeze, and the water rippled slightly where the top of my nets broke the surface. I relished the novelty of my situation, sitting there in a dinghy in the middle of a reed bed, with countless frogs and toads for noisy company and with the slowly wheeling stars for illumination. But soon the novelty wore off, and I found it hard to concentrate on my vigil. The seat was uncomfortable and I started to get cramp; when I moved to ease this, the boat scraped against the reeds beneath it, the noise causing the frogs and toads to fall totally silent for a few moments, then resuming their chorus when it became apparent that there was no danger. I yawned and rubbed my eyes, which were becoming dazed by the effort of concentrating in that dim light upon the small patch of disturbed water above the nets. I made great efforts to hold my heavy head upright, but with diminishing success. At about three in the morning I decided fuzzily that I would be more comfortable if I lay down in the dinghy, on the duck-boards between the seats, and there continued my vigil, keeping very carefully awake. . .

The next thing I knew was that my name was being shouted at me from the far bank downstream; also, that the sun was high and already hot. I sprang to my feet, almost capsizing the dinghy, and called out weakly to show where I was. No evasions, no excuses were possible: the sentry had fallen asleep at his post. I slid the dinghy out from the reed bed and over to the nets, sheepishly admitting to Robert that I wouldn't be able to hold down a job as a night watchman. He was standing there on the opposite bank, with his guns and his dogs, and if it hadn't been for the big bush hat he was wearing, the whole picture would have suggested an English squire going out on a duck shoot and coming across the lair of a guilty poacher.

I had caused them some worry. By the time the sun had been up for two hours without any sign of my return, they had begun to think that the dinghy had capsized or that I had otherwise contrived to drown myself. I explained, lamely, that I had stayed awake until three o'clock at least. But when we had a look at the nets, it became obvious that my shameful weakness had caused me to miss a real chance. There were a few dead fish in the nets, and also two large and expensive holes. While I was sleeping so peacefully two otters must have come for the fish and become entangled in the nets, but then had had all the time in the world to bite themselves free with their razor-sharp teeth. I was grieved: Robert laughed. Then we went back to camp empty-handed, and on the way we saw the dinosaur-like form of a big water monitor as it slid from the bank into the security of the reeds. It was a good five feet long. Water monitors are larger than their land-loving cousins, the rock monitors, and can grow to as much as ten feet, three-fifths of which, are accounted for by the tail. On dry land they can move well but not very rapidly, and although they have no webbing between their toes, they are excellent swimmers, using their long powerful tails: I felt rather glad that it had not decided to climb into the dinghy while I slept.

One might have expected that after this failure – which was not my first – my reputation as a trapper of wild animals would be somewhat diminished. But no, almost at once I was enlisted to help in a serious crisis. I visited the Calvers to have another look at my spur-winged geese, and Dave Calver told me that for the last four nights they had been troubled by an aardvark which had come into the garden, chosen the best of the flower beds, and had dug into it most destructively. Each morning they repaired the damage as best they could and even fenced off that flower bed with branches and wire; but each night the aardvark came back and did it again. On the fourth night Dave stationed one of his Africans to keep an all-night vigil; 'But would you believe it,' he told me, 'the fellow fell asleep on the job!'

'Shocking,' I replied, 'outrageous.'

'So you're the right man to help.'

I seemed to be stuck with the job, and I pondered over its difficulties. How on earth *do* you catch an aardvark which has buried itself in a flower bed? I had read that this animal, with its powerful claws, can dig itself into soft earth quicker than men with spades can follow. Could I grab hold of it above ground-level? I had been told of an African who had tried this and had been pulled down the aardvark's burrow up to his waist even though two men were holding his legs: if he hadn't let go he would have been pulled right down into the animal's network of underground tunnels.

I returned to camp and asked for Robert's and June's advice. June suggested, not too seriously, that we should use Chinky, who would be glad of some aardvark meat. Dogs might be more practical; but I knew that Henry would be off like a shot if confronted with any such grotesque creature as this. It would have to be human cleverness once again, deployed quickly: I had promised the Calvers to solve their problem on the next day.

Robert's suggestion was a pit-trap: they had made one a few years ago in order to catch some lion cubs, which they had photographed and then released. He drew me a diagram: it was an elaborate affair, a large pit with a collapsible roof, covered over with earth, triggered off by a pull on a rope. But this wasn't the easiest sort of answer. For one thing, it would be a major operation, quite destroying the flower bed that the Calvers wanted to preserve. Then, we would have to line the pit very strongly: otherwise the animal, when trapped, would simply dig down and be as inaccessible as ever. And what would we do with the aardvark when we had caught it? I didn't want it for my collection, and in any case, I had no cage strong enough to hold such a powerful digger.

Even so we decided that this was the only workable answer. So next morning we set off for the Calvers, with John and another African well armed with digging implements.

Dave greeted us jubilantly. 'I've saved you a little bit of trouble,' he said. 'I shot the thing from the verandah in the early hours of this morning, so my wife's flower bed will soon be back to normal.'

My first reaction to this news was one of pure relief; then, when I was shown the aardvark's body, I felt sorry for it. I had never seen one before, and I studied it with interest: the hunched massive body, with its long head and snout, and the round blunt pig-like muzzle with its big round nostrils; the tubular ears, that move independently and can be folded down to exclude dirt while the animal is burrowing; the tapering tongue and the similarly tapering tail; the short stocky legs with their power-ful claws. I could well understand the animal's effectiveness as an excavator. The name aardvark means, literally, 'earth-pig'; but this creature, with its dull yellowish-grey body, looked more alien and remote than any pig in my experience.

Relieved of that task, we went back to camp and relaxed. Just below the bridge over the Thamalakane, there was a stretch of river where the east bank was clear of weeds, where we could therefore dive and swim in the crystal-clear waters without any danger of being ambushed by lurking crocodiles. We used to visit this swimming place daily, going there some-times by truck, sometimes by dinghy. It was my own pleasure to take the inner tube of a tyre and lie cradled in it, floating gently upon the water, staring at the sky, and watching a pied kingfisher that haunted the spot. It seemed almost tame; it was quite undeterred by our presence, and in fact seemed to delay its hunting until we arrived. Our swimming and splash-ing would disturb the fish and drive them out to the nearby shallows, where the kingfisher could get at them more easily. It would hover there above the water, then suddenly flash down like an arrow, coming up a moment later with a fish: I felt rather glad that there wasn't any bird big enough to play the same game with my inner tube and my defenceless person.

Eventually Chinky's travelling-cage arrived, delivered at the camp by Riley's Transport. It was a heavy metal cage, need-ing two men to carry it, and perhaps six (I thought) when Chinky was inside. Robert examined it carefully and studied the workings of the sliding door at the end; and then he told me that it could be loaded on to the back of the DUKW. The point was that until I was ready to leave the district with Chinky, this cage would serve as a trap: we could take it with us, and possibly catch a number of larger animals, when we set forth on the journey to the northern regions that was going to be the next stage in my adventures.

CHAPTER 7

Lions, Lions and More Lions

IT took us two days to pack all that we would need during
our stay in the northern regions of the Okavango swamps.
We had three vehicles. Robert was to drive the DUKW,
loaded up with all my boxes and cages and frames and nets,
and carrying Timmy as a cabin-passenger; June was to drive
the diesel truck, with Kisi and two other Africans as her
passengers, and with the twelve brown hens crated and
stowed in the back; I was to drive the old Dodge truck, with
John as my passenger and with Chinky in the back. To complete the procession, there was a well-seasoned grey horse,
which Robert had just bought and which a local Batawana
guide had agreed – in a rash moment – to ride.

My collection – apart from Chinky – was to be left in the
care of the African who was staying behind to look after the
camp. Now, and for about the hundredth time, I ran over
his instructions for the proper care of the teal, the python,
and the gerbil, and promised him a good *bonseller* if everything was all right when I came back. A member of the local
veterinary department agreed to call in from time to time
and make sure that all the animals were all right: this eased my
anxieties a good deal.

And so we formed up and set forth, with Robert giving
the starting signal from the cockpit of the DUKW: I felt a
sense of excitement and occasion as our parade moved in
order out of camp, the grey horse first, then Robert, then
June, and myself in the rear. It was a noisy parade; the

DUKW, in particular, made a terrible racket, scattering the wildlife, with fleeing wildebeest and zebra visible from time to time. We kept a good distance between the vehicles, since the ground was often sandy and needed to be negotiated at a good speed, by the trucks at least. The DUKW could look after itself: it had a low-geared six-wheel drive that could negotiate any sort of country, and it also had a winch at the back. Provided that there was something to attach the cable to, it could winch itself out of any sticky spot.

For the first part of the journey we stuck to the well-established track which led in a north-easterly direction towards the village of Mababe. On this track we could maintain a steady ten miles an hour. But after four hours we left it and took a more northerly course into a more isolated and uninhabited region. Here the going was tougher. At times we had to stop and cut back some of the branches of the mopane trees so that the DUKW could get through. When things got really difficult, our mounted guide would go ahead and find the best route for us to take.

We were travelling across country, not following the winding courses of the waterways, and through a rather featureless landscape, in which it would be easy to get lost. As a precaution we made a practice of blazing trees as we went by, thus making it easier to retrace our steps if necessary.

It was in this kind of country that we halted for our first night out, setting up camp by a small water-hole that was covered with a carpet of weed. The spaniels insisted on drinking thirstily from this stagnant looking pond, although they had already been given some safer water. We fed the lions, we fed the brown hens, and then we fed ourselves, with Kisi doing the cooking over a campfire.

To any African who might have come upon us unexpectedly, our camp would have presented a strange and unnerving sight: the trucks, the tank-like bulk of the DUKW, the people and the lions among them. In the event we were ignored by man and beast, with just two exceptions. The numerous tsetse fly were extremely glad to see us, and gave us a welcome which could not be controlled by the use of the fly-swat or by my own chewing of garlic. This was our bad luck. The whole of this area to the north of Maun is considered to be a tsetse-fly area, but they do not occupy the whole of it: they appear to concentrate upon certain stretches of bush, which cannot be identified in advance. Only experience could tell us whether we had chanced to pitch our camp in one of these occupied areas or not. On this first night, we had.

Then there were lions in the region; and of course we had a very charming lady lion with us. After her dinner, perhaps realising that she was back in the wilds, Chinky started her full-throated roaring: four deep drawn-out bellows, and then three shorter descending notes, and then all over again. At first Timmy replied, with a rather pathetic flat howl, but Chinky ignored him and he soon shut up. We went to bed; but in the early hours of the morning I was woken up by further loud roaring from Chinky, and then heard in the distance the deep answering reply of a wild male. This would not do: when sleeping out in the open, you don't want an untamed and amorous lion prowling around your camp. So I went over to the truck and had a few quiet soothing words with Chinky, begging her to keep a maidenly silence. Fortunately she agreed, and together we listened in silence to the receding roars of the disappointed suitor.

Next day we set out again through more of that mopane shrubland and then over open veldt until we arrived at the Machabe River, sometimes called the Kwaai. Chinky was very much on the alert now, and took a deep interest in her new surroundings: for her sake I was pleased at this, but I was less pleased when in her excitement she started to swing her heavy person from side to side in the truck, thus altering its balance and causing it to swerve rather dangerously. This added to John's nervousness: he kept looking back through the small cab window to see where Chinky was, fearing that some extra violent swerve or jolt might throw her forward into the cab and on top of him.

We travelled along the south bank of the river, keeping

carefully to the firm ground, well away from the tall reed beds: it was rather like driving through a lonely region of the Norfolk Broads. Robert was looking for a crossing-place; eventually we found one where, by laying branches and reeds in the tracks made by the DUKW, we could provide a surface across which the lighter trucks could cross without getting stuck. So we crossed the river and went on, and arrived at what Robert and June called Fig Tree Camp. It was a beautiful place, with two fig trees standing alone in the middle of some dry veldt, a most pleasant change from the scruffy disorder of the mopane shrubland. We set up camp under the fig trees, with the veldt sloping down before us to the reed beds and the crystalline waters of the river. It was as though we were in a country mansion, looking out at the park and the lake, well stocked with ornamental waterfowl.

Here the tsetse fly were few and far between: even the nocturnal mosquitoes were as considerate as was their nature to be. A flock of spur-winged geese flew past along the line of the river, their long black necks and bodies thrusting through the air like jet fighters, their formation a perfect V, up to the highest standards of an RAF ceremonial fly-past.

Robert lifted Timmy down from the DUKW and exercised him, using a collar and a long chain, afterwards tethering him with a strong metal peg in the shade of the nearby shrub. I was tempted to give Chinky also some measure of freedom, since her accommodation in the truck was cramped; but the danger was too great. She was all too likely to go off on a honeymoon with one of the local lads, and thus miss her appointment to travel to Jersey with me. I explained this to her as best I could, while engaged in cleaning her out and covering the floor of the truck with fresh reeds. This confinement was temporary, I told her, and so was her celibacy: she was in fact betrothed to a very good-looking lion which had been at the Jersey Zoo for the last three years and would doubtlessly prove to have all the charm and blarney of the Irish, since he had been born in the Dublin Zoo. She licked the back of my hand with her rough tongue when she heard this, just as if she understood everything and would be faithful and save herself for marriage.

Alas! Good resolutions often go down before the stormy forces of nature. On our third night at Fig Tree Camp she came into season, forgot the voice of conscience, and set about making quite sure that every male lion in the Okavango knew of her presence and loneliness. June at once put the tape-recorder into action, so that we would have an audible souvenir of this trip. I found the noise rather romantic at first: it was certainly a great experience to be sleeping out there in the wilds of Africa, with a real live lion roaring its head off a few yards away. But the old problem recurred, sweeping aside all such sentimentality: we heard a male lion answering Chinky's call, and much closer at hand than the one we had heard before. She continued with her calling, in a voice less plaintive, more compelling and urgent; and then, from another direction, we heard the reply of another male.

Robert came up and spoke to her sharply, rebuking her provocative behaviour and showing her his rifle. No, he wasn't threatening her with death: the point was that she found the deafening report of a gun an unnerving and sobering experience, and therefore respected even the sight of one. The formula worked for a time: she became calmer, and settled down on to her bed of reeds. We relaxed and went back to bed ourselves. But soon we heard the perplexed calls of those two lions once again, and much nearer. Chinky rose to her feet, and before Robert could show her his rifle again, she gave forth the most beseeching roar I have ever heard.

Things were getting out of hand. We put the three apprehensive spaniels into the safety of the DUKW – the bold Henry was quaking in terror, so that I could hardly hold him – and prepared for action. June came out of the cabin of her truck with a Verey pistol at the ready, and climbed up and stood on top looking around. It was a fine clear night; we had a good view over the veldt and down to the river. We awaited developments.

Soon we heard a startled wail from Timmy, who was about fifteen paces behind the DUKW, and when we looked we caught a quick glimpse of the eyes of a lion on a game-trail in the bush behind him. They disappeared at once into the shadows of the mopane: the wild lion had been expecting to find a female, and his encounter with Timmy must have been equally unexpected on both sides. But we couldn't take risks: we decided to bring Timmy right into the middle of the camp as quickly as possible. June switched on the small 80-watt light that was mounted on top of the DUKW and started to sweep the surrounding bush with its beam: Robert persuaded two of the Afrcians to climb down from their place of safety and rekindle the fire into a blaze. Chinky gave a few faint sounds, but was silenced utterly when Robert fired his rifle into the air. Now, perhaps, Timmy could be fetched in. Robert walked in his direction, while June and I kept him covered with searchlight and rifle respectively: he was approaching the point where the wild lion had been seen. Then we heard Timmy's welcoming noise and he came bounding back into the light of the camp fire, with Robert holding the chain.

Chinky was on her feet again, swaying from side to side, her eyes fixed on the direction from which Timmy had just been fetched. In the distance we heard the call of a hyena, which obviously thought that the lions must have made a kill and was hunting for the carcase. We needed to strengthen our position; so we tethered Timmy and the grey horse at opposite ends of the DUKW and arranged all three vehicles so as to make a sort of triangular stockade, with the camp fire in the middle. But Chinky resumed her amorous roaring, despite some hard words from us and another deafening rifle shot from Robert. The wild lions seemed unlikely to go away.

It was not easy to decide what to do. Chinky herself was in no danger, imprisoned within the strongly-built Dodge truck; but if the lions came for her, Timmy and the horse would be in danger of being attacked. Our own position was not altogether safe.

For a while there was silence. Then it was broken by the simultaneous roar of two lions, very close at hand; Chinky answered, and was answered in her turn from an even shorter distance. Then, in the beam of the searchlight, we saw the emerald gleam of four eyes. Robert fired a warning shot over their heads, and they disappeared at once into the mopane on our left. There was silence again, and then the barking of some baboons not far away, disturbed by the noise of the rifle. I could hear branches snapping in the bush, telling us where the lions had gone: Chinky was straining her eyes in that direction, and soon – yet again – she had started up on her anthems of love.

There was nothing we could do except keep guard all night. June continued to sweep our surroundings with the searchlight, and Robert and I sat vigilant, rifles across our knees, looking (I suppose) rather like the sheriff's posse in some doubtful Western. Our Africans certainly looked as though they had just survived one attack from the Comanches and could expect another at any moment. Time ticked by: Chinky kept up her lovesong, but with less and less conviction and with no further result, until – just as the first touches of dawn lit up the sky – she gave it up, sank down, and went to sleep.

We didn't want another night of that kind, but while Chinky remained in her present loving mood, there wasn't much that we could do. The main thing was to shift the locality of our camp, removing it to more open ground, so that any courting male lion – or any predator, for that matter – would have to cross a good area of open veldt before reaching us. So, while Chinky slept peacefully and enviably, we set about packing our recently unloaded gear and moving. By lunchtime we had found the right place: it was still close to the Kwaai River, but with no bush or other real cover within a quarter of a mile. We arranged the three vehicles in the same defensive triangle, and then set about surrounding the camp with branches, thus erecting a barrier which any lion would need to jump before reaching us. But as we had chosen the site for its remoteness from cover, this meant that the branches had to be dragged a quarter of a mile before being put in place. The operation almost brought us to our knees: dinner, that night, was served to a very exhausted camp.

We made a point of giving Chinky a really enormous meal. Then (we hoped) she would fall into the deep sleep of repletion: alternatively, the pains of indigestion might divert her thoughts from love. And in fact she did behave rather better that night, with just a few enticing roars, these being halfheartedly answered from afar. No doubt the wild lions felt they had seen through her: she was plainly a decoy, set up to draw them into some kind of human devilry. But we couldn't rely on this: they might come back. So Robert and I decided to take it in turns to watch over the camp, with two Africans taking it in turns to keep the fire blazing, while the rest caught up on their sleep – on top of the DUKW in the case of the Africans, though Robert and I slept on the ground.

This exhausting routine went on for four days, sapping our energies and making it impossible for us to make a start on my collection. It was really tiresome of Chinky, and we did feel exasperated with her, but never for very long: her charm could soothe away anybody's resentments and irritations, and she never lost her temper. We forgave her. But I found myself reflecting upon what the novelists and the poets have told us about the disruptive and shattering effect of love upon the female: seldom (I felt) can there have been a more painful example.

Eventually we started to move around. We had brought the aluminium dinghy with us, strapped to the top of the diesel truck: we fitted the outboard motor to this, and so we were able to explore up and down the Kwaai. The rainy season had started, but the water level was still very low indeed. The bird life was much the same as I had seen on the Thamalakane, but without the multi-coloured pygmy geese: it seemed also that the cormorants had been replaced, here, by the goliath heron, large birds that went about in pairs, not in flocks as the

Under the discerning eyes of the Hon Director of the Jersey Wildlife Preservation Trust or learning about seriemas from Gerald Durrell.

Beauty and the beast.

cormorants had done. On one occasion I saw a saddle-billed stork standing alone, the yellow saddle on its beak suggesting the squadron badge on the nose of a fighter aircraft. It took off and flew away purposefully, as though to a defined target.

My first capture – I should rather call it my first find, since no pursuit or trapping was involved – was a Bell's hinged tortoise. I carried it back to our camp and showed it to Chinky, who begged me to give it to her to play with. Henry rushed up and barked at it: Gilly-Anne was close behind him, and he needed to seem tough and aggressive, he therefore plucked up enough courage to sniff at it timidly, growling at the same time, as though to warn it not to start any tricks.

I selected the lushest area of grass within our camp area and made a wire enclosure. This was useless: I hadn't realised how well tortoises could climb. This one, with its horny legs, functioned like a small climbing tank, and it was up and across those eighteen inches of wire in no time, so that I had to find closer accommodation for it. In this species, the bottom shell or plastron is hinged in front like the bows of a landing-craft, and closes up to protect the head in any emergency. Examining my specimen, I found that the surface of the plastron was distinctly concave. In tortoises this is a mark of maleness: the plastron is concave so as to accommodate the top shell or carapace of the female during copulation. I thus had a male tortoise on my hands, and I decided to call him Albert after my grandfather, and to find him a mate if possible.

Robert now came forward with a somewhat hair-raising suggestion. 'You have often told us about that crocodile in the Jersey Zoo,' he said, 'how it likes having its neck scratched. Well, how about catching a companion for it? How about this evening?'

This prospect shook me a little: Robert was a bit too keen on any scheme that promised entertainment. It is one thing to scratch a crocodile with a stick through a slit in a glass door: it is quite another thing to venture out into the swamps at night and fling your arms about an unknown saurian and carry it away, despite all protest. But Robert swept aside my

145

I

misgivings and started off on explanations and arrangements. The main thing, he told me, was to pick up a young one and not an adult: the thing to note was the distance between the reptile's eyes. In the dark, this would give you a clue to its size.

Crocodiles, like alligators and gharials, belong to a very old family which can trace its ancestry right back to Jurassic times, some 140 or 170 million years ago. They are all amphibious and egg-laying and they feed mainly on fish, but they do catch mammals as well, and sometimes man. The Nile crocodile, which is the species found in the Okavango swamps, can reach a length of sixteen feet; it is the baby of the family, since the Mississippi alligator is known to reach nineteen feet and two inches, and the Orinoco crocodile has been recorded at over twenty-three. I was glad that we were not going out after these larger reptiles.

That night turned out to be unusually dark, which was useful, as it would enable us to come right up close to the crocodiles before being seen. We pushed the dinghy out into the river and droned away, the noise of the outboard motor silencing the music of the frogs: I attended to the motor, Kisi sat amidships, and Robert knelt in the bows to guide us. He had a powerful torch fixed to the front of his bush hat: this left his hands free to gather up crocodiles. The beam from the torch swept the dark surface of the water as we went, and Robert kept his eyes ahead, alert to catch the reflection of the light in a crocodile's eyes.

He had to watch out for something else as well: at any moment we might see the mountainous form of a hippopotamus, browsing in the reed beds at night. If it were alarmed it would probably come crashing back into the safety of the deeper water, which would not be healthy for our frail dinghy: and if we met it head on in some narrow channel, we would have to turn about very sharply, since these big creatures will not reverse. Altogether, I hoped that we would not meet a hippopotamus that night. But I was grieved to hear that they were becoming scarcer and disappearing from their old haunts. This had practical disadvantages. When the hippo was plentiful people did not fully realise that by bulldozing his way through the reed beds and following the water in the dry season, he provided a free dredging and irrigation service. Where he has disappeared many of the lesser waterways have become silted up and good pasture lands have thus been deprived of water.

A refreshing breeze prevented the ubiquitous mosquitoes from settling on our skin. We puttered on, and in the moving beam of the torch we saw a continuous diving display, given by frogs and toads of every shape and size as they leapt off the water-lily leaves on our approach. Robert gesticulated like a French policeman, guiding us in what he hoped was the right direction; and, sure enough, we soon sensed an extra excitement in his movements. When I turned the boat to port, as indicated, I saw two reptilian eyes reflecting the beam of the torch. I now had to bring the dinghy up close, so that Robert could grab hold of the crocodile as we went by: fortunately it seemed to be hypnotised by the torchlight, and there was a pounce and a splash and a spraying of water from the flailing tail as Robert swung the creature over and dropped it neatly into the awaiting box.

'Your turn now,' he said, and we carefully changed places. In the dark I saw a white flash of teeth: Kisi was grinning sympathetically, doubtlessly glad that it was not he who had to make the attempt. I strapped the torch to my jungle hat, feeling rather like a coalminer about to descend a flooded pit to rescue a comrade: I tried to build up my morale by thinking of the loneliness of that crocodile back at home in Jersey, but I didn't care very much at this time. But I pointed ahead bravely, as a signal to Robert to proceed, and tried to remember my instructions. If the eyes are far apart, leave it alone: it's a big specimen. If they're close together it will be a small one and easy to manage, as we had just seen. But what if there were two big ones side by side, their inner eyes close together? And in any case, how can you assess the distance between the eyes when you don't know (because of the dark) how far away the creature is? Two reassuringly close eyes could widen alarmingly on a closer approach, and it might be too late by then. 'Oh well,' I said to myself in resigned fashion, as the motor puttered away behind me and my torch played over these dangerous waters, 'perhaps I'll get away cheaply and just lose my fingers.' That would mean an end to my piano-playing – a sad thing for me, but possibly in the public interest.

It was altogether too much of a gamble, too much like Russian roulette. What a fool I had been to consent to this rash game! But being now committed, I could hardly back out. Henry was always trying to appear heroic in Gilly-Anne's eyes, and here was I trying to appear heroic in Robert's eyes: for dog or for man, the fear of appearing cowardly can over-rule all other fears.

Forests of reeds slid by on either side, and there was that steady plunging and plopping of amphibians in the torchlight. I started to relax, thinking joyfully that the riparian version of a bush telegraph must have told all the crocodiles that there were kidnappers abroad, so that they had gone into hiding. But then, suddenly and with mixed feelings, I saw two icy eyes straight ahead.

I flapped my hands wildly, like a learner driver making a hand-signal, and kept the spotlight upon the animal's head. Robert must have seen it too: he brought the boat alongside with effortless precision. Did I try to assess the distance between the eyes? I can't remember, but presumably Robert would have warned me if I were trying to haul a twelve-footer aboard. I just remember plunging my hand into the cool water, aiming at a point about two inches behind the eyes and allowing for refraction: my hand made contact with the cold slimy shoulders, and my fingers closed over them tightly. At once the crocodile took fright and started to flail around: I clung and wrestled, and managed to swing it up and over the gunwale of the dinghy in the nick of time. As it came over it wriggled out of my grip and fell into the bottom of the boat, where it created a certain amount of chaos: Kisi very nearly abandoned ship, but remembered in time that there would be other crocodiles in the water. In the dark I could not see where my captive had got to: I wrenched the torch off my hat to see, and Robert went into efficient action and cornered the angry beast under the duck-boards by his seat. I opened the box that already held one specimen and Robert firmly put the second inside, then closed the box firmly. We breathed again, and I felt a certain sense of achievement. I was to blame for stupidly dropping my crocodile, but at least I had managed to catch it, and it hadn't got away.

Like the hippopotamus the crocodile is now becoming some-what rare, and is hard to find outside such isolated places as these Okavango swamps: too many of them have been shot or trapped so that the skin from the belly can be made into such luxury articles as ladies' handbags, wallets, and shoes. In this age of synthetics it is quite inexcusable to bring a wild animal close to extinction for the pleasure of having its beautiful skin. A good plastic substitute can be made easily enough. Failing this, if the human race insists on authenticity, then breeding colonies could be maintained for the purpose, so that the wild stock can remain unmolested and undiminished. We have done this with the chinchilla, the mink, the coypu, and some others: we should do it with the crocodile as well – an interesting and archaic animal which will soon be nothing but a memory, if the present rate of killing continues.

The moon now slid out from behind a blanket of rain clouds, and we turned back for camp by its light, speeding past those diving frogs at full throttle, the propeller churning up the water like a kitchen mixer. On three separate occasions we had to stop and tip up the outboard motor to clear the propeller of weeds: then, with a pull on the cord, we would be on our way again, down the winding river, until we arrived back at our camp just after midnight. The crocodiles were quite motionless in their box as Kisi and I carried them ashore, and even when we showed them to Henry, who barked at them terribly, they remained as though frozen.

At first light the following morning, I put John on to

making a holding cage for the two now, very stern looking crocodiles. I designed the cage in such a way that the cage's bottom and ends were made of wire, so that when it was placed amongst the cool of the reeds, and angled correctly, the crocodiles had the choice of either being partially submerged in water, or being able to remain on dry land. They would also be able to take advantage of eating any fish or amphibian life that came their way. Both the specimens were between 2 and 3 feet long, and as young crocodiles develop rapidly during their early years, they were probably both still under five years old. Although I knew that it was comparatively easy to sex crocodilians, by simply feeling within the anus as to whether a penis is present or not, I decided not to trust my luck too far, after dropping the specimen I had handled during the capturing operation.

I now turned my attention to carrion-eating birds. There were plenty of these: I had left some meat around to attract their attention, and through my binoculars I had seen three species of vulture, one tawny eagle, many parsonical-looking marabou storks, and also (to vary the theme) a black-backed jackal. I therefore decided that a representative collection of carrion-eaters – of birds especially – would add to my collection on very interesting lines. This is an aspect of African wildlife which everybody has seen in films and read about in books. Whenever an animal dies, a kind of natural public health and sanitation department goes into action at once: the jackals, the hyenas, the vultures, the marabou storks all play their part in disposing of the flesh and the bones, while the dung beetles and other insects clear up the excreta. Soon there is only a rather trampled patch of ground to show where some animal has recently died.

And so, after our night with the crocodiles, we sat and discussed the matter over a good breakfast. Our twelve brown hens were well established in the camp and provided us with plenty of large brown eggs. We ate some of these, drank coffee made from Nescafé and evaporated milk, and considered the capture of carrion-eaters. Our kit included a reel of strong fishing gut, too thin for a bird to see easily, and from this we planned to make a number of loops or nooses. These could be attached to tins or cans, filled with earth and therefore very heavy, and arranged in a big circle around the place where we proposed to put out some meat as bait. The plan depended upon the birds' habits. They would land some thirty or forty feet away from the carrion and then approach it with their customary and very ungainly prancing motion. Thus, we hoped, they would get their feet caught in these nooses; and if they tried to take off and fly away, they would be held down by the heavy tins. I would then be able to break cover, sprint a hundred yards, and clasp the captives to my bosom.

It was an obviously sound plan, and we set to work. We decided to bury the cans which anchored our nooses, so as to make them less conspicuous and more secure: Robert helped me in this work, but the spaniels were not helpful at all, since they insisted on digging up each can as soon as we had buried it. We had to imprison them in camp for the duration. Chinky seemed anxious to take part in the adventure, but had to be refused; perhaps for the same reason Timmy ran out to grab me by the ankle – just in play, Robert told me – but was fortunately restrained by his chain. Robert gave me a big wildebeeste haunch that came from an animal shot for food, and we placed this in the centre of our circle and retreated into a small copse – alive with tsetse fly – to await developments.

Soon through my binoculars, I saw the first vultures approaching and circling, their great wings flapping slowly. When the first of them landed, I saw that they were immature specimens of the white-headed vulture. It all went as we expected, but only for a time: they pranced along the ground towards the meat and became duly entangled in my gut snares, but then, after a moment's flap and panic, they shook them off easily and flew away. We decided to repeat the experiment, and rearranged the whole trap and the bait on another site. Their suspicions had now been aroused, and it was quite a long time before they came. They were plainly on the look-out for the thin gut; and when one of them touched it with its talon, it gave the alarm and they all flew away. We could lure them to our trap, but not catch them.

I gathered up my useless equipment and went dejectedly back to camp with my African helpers, who had been watching my methods with some incredulity. Then our Batawana guide came up and broke the silence which he had maintained so far: if we liked, he told us, he would demonstrate the method which he would use in such a case.

He cut a sapling and stuck it into the ground. About eighteen inches away from its base he stuck into the ground a staple-shaped piece of wood, surrounding this with small twigs arranged in a circle. He then made twine from long grass, tied one end of it to the top of the sapling, and divided the other end. One part of it became a noose, held in place by that circle of twigs; the other part was attached to a short stick to serve as a trip or catch. Then he bent the spring sapling down, fixing it with a forked twig under the wooden staple. The bait was to be attached to this twig: when the greedy bird tugged at it, the sapling would be released and would straighten upwards, thus drawing the noose tightly round the bird's neck and securing it.

It looked to me like a totally obvious trap, unlikely to fool even the most dim-witted and careless bird. Still, after my own method had failed so miserably, I thought it was worth a try. So on the following day, under the guidance of our Batawana tutor, we set up five of these traps, baiting each with a portion of the meat. As before, we then retreated into the cover of some nearby bushes, and watched the slow suspicious assembly of the vultures and the marabou storks. Some perched doubtfully on a rotten tree nearby, hunched up like witches, before landing heavily: soon quite a number were approaching the carrion, their wings still outspread, their gait still with that awkward prancing character. They did not all come at the same speed. There were poor-spirited specimens which hung back, and there were bolder spirits that pressed forward. It was one of these, naturally enough, that first touched the bait; and the trap sprang itself at once, the noose tightening so that the bird was firmly tethered.

I sprinted forward and seized it, despite its struggles. At once the other birds launched themselves into the air, some of them lightening themselves for easier flight by vomiting up the heavy mass of food that they had already eaten. I grabbed my vulture's neck with my right hand and got its flapping wings under control with my left; then I tucked it firmly under my left arm with its head to the rear, released the noose, and made the bird helpless by holding its legs together.

This was a considerable moral victory for our Batawana guide: I decided to consult him in future about all questions of trapping. Back at our camp I handed the now quiescent bird into June's tender care, and John and I set about making a cage for it. We fixed six of our medium-sized wire frames together, lining all but the bottom and the front side with a protective padding of hessian; and across the middle of this cage I arranged a perch, devised to suit the width of the vulture's talons, so that he could take his ease in his own familiar way. We put this cage on top of a rough table that we had already constructed from branches, and I took the bird from June and slid it inside. At first it lay motionless on the floor as though dead. Then after a few minutes it got up and rushed at the padded sides repeatedly; then, realising that it was trapped, it climbed on to the perch and sat there in a posture of hunched resignation.

I consulted my reference books and decided that this was a specimen of the white-backed vulture, which was common in the tropical savannah bushveldt. Its whitish head was almost devoid of feathers, and its neck resembled that of a partially plucked turkey. Vultures' feet are not adapted to the holding of a live victim, as are those of most birds of prey; their great weapon is the powerful beak, which is perfectly adapted to the tearing of skin and flesh from dead carcases. In some of the regions where they live carcases have become scarce owing to the establishment of European farming methods; and in that situation, being desperate, vultures have been known to attack live sheep. But they have only succeeded in injuring the sheep, not in killing them: unlike the eagles, they are quite unpractised and incompetent in the art of killing.

During the next ten days I concentrated on catching as many different species as I could. The traps succeeded wonderfully, perhaps because they were made wholly out of materials that the birds were accustomed to seeing every day, whereas their keen eyesight would lead them to avoid my fish-gut or anything else unfamiliar. I thus caught two more of the white-backed variety, and then – on a single morning – two specimens of the smaller white-headed vulture. I didn't want too many specimens of any single variety, however, and this meant that I had to release a good many of the birds I caught. This was never understood by John and the other Africans: there I was, spending laborious days in the hot sun in order to catch birds, and then releasing most of those I did catch. As at many other times, my activities must have seemed somewhat crazy to them. The moral is that we should not pass hasty judgement when other people's activities seem crazy to us.

Beyond any doubt the prize of my vulture collection was a fine eared or lappet-faced vulture, the largest species to be found in this area, with a wing-span of over nine feet. June named him after Helen of Troy's Paris, since in her estimation he looked so magnificent. This is a relatively unsociable species, found in twos and threes where others gather by the score; but even so they dominate, driving off competitors until they have chosen the best parts of a carcase, and then standing back to allow the lower classes their turn.

Soon there was a line of cages on that table behind the DUKW. The spaniels gave it a wide berth, no doubt thinking it beneath the dignity of pedigree dogs to associate with such scruffy birds. Chinky also seemed a bit negative about them. They were usually downwind from her truck, so that she couldn't smell them, but if I came straight from handling them to be sociable with her, she would utterly refuse to lick my hand or play patty-paw. Robert felt similarly: he found these carrion-eating birds entertaining but smelly, and moved his camp-bed to place the greatest possible distance between himself and their cages.

With so many large birds on hand we soon ran out of wire frames and hessian, and had to improvise cages, using the straightest branches we could find in the adjacent bush. We allocated ten days to this part of the expedition, and before our time was up I had caught three marabou storks and – an unexpected guest – a tawny eagle. He was nasty to handle. I had no difficulty in extracting a vulture or stork from a trap, but when I came to remove this eagle, he was in an angry mood and lay flat on his back, using his sharp-taloned claws to dangerous effect. Before I could release him and bring him under control, I had to tear off my shirt and press it upon him, so as to give those fierce talons something to hold.

Unfortunately I had not observed the tawny eagle among the vultures before it was caught: I did not know whether it had come along for a share in the meat, or to attack the vultures. I knew that such birds will often attack other birds, as well as hares and small antelopes and other mammals; I had not heard of them attacking carrion-eaters, but I did not want to take risks, and so I housed my eagle separately, well away from the vultures and out of their sight, close to the crocodiles and Albert the tortoise, all of which seemed quite indifferent to their neighbours.

This excellent collection was endangered by a tendency, on the part of some of the birds, to go on hunger-strike. I eventually persuaded them to eat by hanging gory meat in festoons from the roofs of their cages, so that it brushed against their faces and beaks: this irritated them, they snapped at it, found it edible, and fed themselves at last. When they had eaten, the crop of each bird would bulge as

though it had swallowed a cricket-ball. When they were in
that state, it was important not to disturb them: if they
were frightened, their hunched forms would lurch up and
down and they would regurgitate their rations in a definitely
un-beautiful way. I soon learnt this lesson, and learnt also
to feed Chinky and Timmy before the vultures. At first I
failed to do this; and just as I was congratulating myself on
persuading the vultures to eat at last, Chinky gave a loud
hungry roar, all the birds emptied their crops in alarm and
shook their cages in fruitless attempts at mass flight.

At the end of the fourth week, we saw rain clouds gathering darkly and mountainously on the horizon, and we
realised that the first storm of the rainy season was at hand.
I got John to cut me a stack of reeds to be spread out on
top of 'Death Row', which was June's name for the line of
vulture-cages, and also to cover the accommodation of the
marabou storks, the crocodiles, and Albert the tortoise. We
brought Chinky's truck closer to the fig tree, as well as
Timmy and the grey horse, arranging the three animals in
a triangle around the DUKW: and Robert erected a canvas
lean-to against the southern side of the DUKW, so that our
table and our camp-beds would have some shelter against the
expected downpour.

Just before the storm broke, everything became still and
breathless: a silence like that of a crypt hung over the bush
and the veldt and the reed beds, broken only by Chinky as
she swayed to and fro in her restlessness. Then a gentle breeze
fanned the ground, throwing up eddies of dust and bringing
with it the first big spots of rain; then a clap of thunder
from the north-west heralded the full darkness and power
of a tropical storm. Vast inky clouds moved over us, releasing their torrential loads, splashing the red soil around and
piling the water up on the hard soil before it could soak
away, until streams of mud ran under the DUKW to where
we were sitting under the canvas lean-to, flooding and dirty-
ing everything that was not on the camp-beds or the table.

The thunder crashed and rumbled away, and the lightning

lit up the countryside in vivid erratic flashes. The spaniels huddled nervously under one of the bunks in the DUKW; the lions lay crouched; the big birds hunched themselves up on their perches; the crocodiles lay as motionless as ever; and the grey horse remained fairly calm, since Robert had blindfolded it as a precaution against stampede and flight. If it had run away, its chances of survival would have been small.

It was, I suppose, an inconvenience to be thus flooded and muddied out. But the storm was spectacular, a wonderful thing to experience; and when it was over, the rich moist smell of the earth – after the dusty aridity of the dry season – was a sensuous delight to the nostrils.

CHAPTER 8

A Bush Camp Easter

THROUGHOUT this expedition Robert had been in regular radio contact with Maun. Now, by that means, he heard that the Smeetons had arrived from Francistown and wanted to join us at our camp on the Kwaai. They had been expected, but not until the end of the month. So the District Commissioner agreed to bring them up to where we were, with the help of his own guide, so that they could join us for the Easter weekend that was approaching. He also was interested in seeing what animals I had managed to trap.

The Smeetons and their travels were well known to me by reputation. I had read about Beryl Smeeton's extensive journeyings through China, Japan, Persia and Russia in pre-war days – about how she had ridden over the Andes into Patagonia, driven a van through much of the United States, and walked through Burma during the monsoon; I had read about Miles Smeeton's life in India, where – as a regular army officer – he regarded pig sticking and big-game hunting as better training for jungle warfare than most of the official training exercises. I also knew about the somewhat light hearted attempt that they had both made, with Sherpa Tensing, to climb the 25,460-foot Tirich Mir in the Himalayas. But the thing that had really captured my imagination was Miles's book *Once Is Enough*, in which he described their two epic attempts to sail round Cape Horn, their yacht *Tzu Hang* being turned over and smashed up on each occasion. I am not trying to suggest that I envied them this experience: on the whole, I prefer to keep my feet on dry land. But the Smeetons had been stretched to the full, both mentally and physically, on their first attempt; and after its failure they had been game to come back for a second attempt. I admired that. I felt that we were now to have among us travellers of the epic sort, straight from the pages of the old pioneering books. So I tried to follow the example set by their perseverance and work extra hard, so that when they came they would find a notably better and more comprehensive collection than I had achieved so far.

I took thought, therefore, and remembered that a sandy river-side beach nearby was the daily rendezvous of a pair of hamer-kop or hammerheaded storks. Here, where various game had trodden the reeds down on their way to the water, they would arrive each morning, but always separately, as though trying not to attract attention: then they would strut up and down in the shallows, picking up small fish and insects in a somewhat fastidious manner. They were small brown birds, the backs of their heads having a shaggy appearance, suggesting the more hirsute sort of hippie.

So I erected my last mist-net parallel to the water-line along this beach, and hid in the reeds on the opposite side of the river: at this point it was shallow enough to be waded across if I made a capture. The two hamerkops arrived within five minutes of each other, and were apparently not in the least put out by the presence of the two tall aluminium poles that supported my net. They drank and ate as usual, and then waded up and down before the net, as though they were on guard duty. Then they stopped for a siesta, each balancing on one leg within a foot of the other, heads comfortably tucked beneath wings. This gave me my chance: if I rushed at them now, from across the river, they would obviously fly away from me and so collide inextricably with the net. This crafty plan was no sooner devised than put into execution. Unfortunately, instead of flying away from me, the hamer-kops flew vertically upwards, missing the net altogether and disappearing upstream at a low altitude, uttering a peculiar squeaky whistling sort of cry as they went.

I was sorry to lose them; but it was nice to think that they could now continue undisturbed with what I suspected was an impassioned love affair.

I turned back to the net and saw that I had not failed completely: a giant kingfisher was caught in its central fold. It was a handsomely marked bird, its white chest speckled with chestnut, and it did not at all like being handled: it uttered a loud cry when I took hold of it, though I was very gentle. I took it back to camp and placed it carefully in a sheltered cage. It appeared to settle down immediately: it sat there on its perch looking placid and plump and deeply thoughtful.

It had to be fed; and John's duties, which grew heavier as my collection grew larger, now included the finding of some minnow-sized fish. We put these into a bowl and offered them to the kingfisher, but he wouldn't touch them. When this had happened a few times we realised that forcible feeding was going to be the only way of keeping him alive.

So I asked Robert to hold the bird firmly but gently in both hands, and then I tickled the sides of its beak with a struggling minnow. I hoped that he would grab at it, if only in irritation. But soon the minnow stopped struggling, and I had to put it back in a bucket of water to recuperate. Then, holding the base of the upper mandible with one hand, I slowly forced down the lower mandible and slipped a worm into the kingfisher's mouth. This infuriated him: he didn't merely spit out the worm, he also nipped one of my fingers with his beak, and very painfully, to teach me better manners. An uncontrollable reflex made me wrench my hand away, so sharply that I inadvertently pulled the bird right out of Robert's grasp. My finger was thus set free, but so was the bird: in a second it was lost among the reed beds, gone for ever, another specimen destined to escape my collection.

Robert was sympathetic. 'What about the springhare?' he said. 'It's a handsome beast, and it isn't often seen in European zoos. I'll take you out this evening to catch some.' He said this over lunch, and very casually. These animals, he explained, are easy to catch: get them in the direct beam of the headlights and they'll stay fixed, hypnotised, until someone comes round behind and grabs them by the long ears. This sounded marvellously easy: I got two baskets ready, and prepared for a productive evening.

We made sure that June had a Verey pistol loaded and ready, in case we had to be summoned back for some emergency, and we took the diesel truck and drove off to the rear of the camp until we came to an area of open short grassland, where the soil was particularly sandy. There were no springhares in sight. Robert stopped the truck and told me that they had almost certainly been there, but had bolted down their holes when they heard us coming. If we kept quiet for five minutes, he said, and then switched the headlights on suddenly, we would be sure to see a number of them grazing by their burrows. And so it turned out. We waited in silence: the night air was damp with the moisture that rose from the hot earth, and we heard an owl hooting nearby as it went about the night's hunting. Then Robert pressed the switch, floodlighting the grassy area in front of us and illuminating the kangaroo-like figures of two springhares, which stood there mesmerised and immovable. Silently I slid down from the cab and circled round to approach one of them from behind and also from downwind: surprise would be the key to success.

You never know how uneven these apparently lawn-like grasslands of the bush really are until you try to move over them quickly and silently in the dark, and without any light. I kept stumbling over small ridges and hollows, tripping over bits of vegetation, lacerating my skin on thorny acacia bushes: twice I actually fell, just managing to hold back the loud curses that would have eased my feelings but also broken the spell that held my quarry in a kind of trance. As I rose again I could see it clearly: the cinnamon-buff pelage, the long narrow ears, the big nocturnal eyes that now reflected the truck's headlights. I came closer, losing one of my shoes in my excitement but caring nothing now for any such loss or discomfort: I was right behind the springhare, its ears tilted helpfully in my direction, and then I pounced, swooped like an eagle, and grasped it by the base of the ears and the long back legs. I had to hold it carefully away from me, or the long curved claws on the front feet could have hurt me nastily. Robert drove up, having very much appreciated the performance, and we put the springhare into one of the baskets and started to look for the missing shoe. We never found it; the bush claimed it as the price of my springhare. I had no intention of repeating the exercise in only one shoe, so we went back to camp, resolving to come back next evening to capture a mate for our new friend.

I wanted to see some of the larger wildlife at closer quarters, and I knew that one could approach them more closely on horseback than on foot. So next morning I borrowed the grey mare and set out soon after dawn. She was broad and comfortable, and proceeded in a very curious gait, half trot and half canter, a consequence, probably, of the Africans' refusal to rise in the stirrups while trotting. I was soon rewarded: wildebeest, impala, zebra, warthog, baboon, and sitatunga were to be seen in quantity, all looking as fresh and cheerful as the morning itself. I found a whole family of warthogs wallowing in a mud-bath, smiling as their American cousins, the dangerous peccaries, do: the two young ones had faintly striped reddish-brown bodies, and the parents had the characteristic crest of long black bristles, with large fleshy warts below their eyes. They emerged from their mud-bath deeply refreshed, and then the boar's acute sense of smell and perhaps of hearing told him of my presence. At once his tail flew up as a danger signal and all four stampeded off in great confusion, probably to take refuge in some deserted aardvark burrow and to consider their own rashness in allowing a human being to come so close to them undetected.

Later on, during that same day, Robert and I saw the largest concentration of game that I had ever encountered. We had driven about four miles upriver from camp when quite by chance we came upon a herd of between five and seven hundred wildebeest or brindled gnu. It is gratifying enough to see any animals in the wild state, but it was really astonishing to find a herd of this size, living their own life in total liberty, not even partly fenced in as they would be in a game reserve. This was a totally unspoilt part of Africa.

We moved in slowly towards them, and I felt rather as though I was on a cattle ranch in America's old West. The young wildebeest calves were being suckled by their mothers, and they seemed quite undisturbed by our presence: they frisked their black horse-like tails and butted greedily at the udders. The adults were bearded, and had tufts of long black hair protruding from muzzle and throat and between the forelegs: in their buff to black vestments they looked like dignitaries attending a congress of the Greek Orthodox Church. Henry was in the cab with us, and he was enchanted by the clouds of unusual smells that were coming his way: his nose twitched frenziedly, and he quite forgot to utter the bark with which he usually commented upon such situations.

We watched the herd for a good quarter of an hour, and then Robert restarted the engine and drove slowly forwards, to see how close we could advance without disturbing them. When we were about fifteen yards from the nearest of them a few of the larger wildebeest began to edge in our direction, snorting and pawing the ground in threatening gestures, Henry got the message and threw himself down to the floor of the cab in some terror. Then the herd started to move away, leaving a protective rearguard of a few big specimens which tried to keep us at bay by making menacing little charges, digging at the ground with their horns, snorting, then dashing away, then turning again to face us, their tails thrashing vigorously all the time. The sun had been very hot recently, and the earth had quite dried out after the storm: when the herd began to move more quickly, a great dust storm arose, like a desert sand storm. There must have been a real shortage of water. Wildebeest usually go about in small herds of five to fifteen, based on scattered waterholes. It is only when these dry up that they come snowballing together in search of some major water supply – in this case, the main streams of the Okavango swamps.

On our way back to camp I spotted the large form of a

leopard tortoise. We stopped the truck and took it on board: this was one capture which succeeded without any speed on my part. It was about one and a half feet long, and when I looked at it closely, I saw that it must have been involved in a bush fire at some time: the horny plates or laminae covering the carapace on the left side, had been burned off, exposing part of the undershell. I decided to take it back to camp to see if it could be a companion for Albert. Henry was nervous about having it in the cab, but took some comfort when his challenging growl brought no counter-challenge.

And so we came home, and attempted to repeat the previous evening's success with the springhare, but without success: when we switched on the headlights, after the same five minutes' wait, there was not a specimen to be seen. We knew that they were around, since we had seen them momentarily on our drive out to the place, appearing before us and vanishing at once. But they didn't seem anxious to fall for the same method. Maybe the word had got around.

I was very much enjoying my stay out in the wilds, but I noticed that John was unhappy: compared with what he had been used to it was a lonely existence for him. He used to follow me around like a devoted disciple, and always looked anxious when I felt the camp without him. But he had settled down well to his duties, which he had restricted to the preparation of the vultures' food, the cutting of reeds for Chinky's flooring, and the catching of a few fish. He was willing to feed the tortoises with greenstuffs, but apart from that he left the feeding of the livestock entirely to me, himself keeping apart and well away from any possible danger. He was homesick, which would not have surprised me in a town-dweller, but did surprise me in him, since he came from a very similar countryside: during the last ten days of our stay by the Kwaai, he seemed to ask me every day when we would be going back to Mazoe.

For my part, I would have been ready to spend any amount of time there in the Okavango, observing the wildlife and its infinitely varied behaviour. A morning ride on the grey horse was now part of my daily routine, and a very enjoyable one: it made me feel as close to nature as I could possibly get, and filled me with tranquillity and satisfaction.

There was always something new to see. Sometimes I would come across a small collection of the dull greyish-brown sita- tunga, feeding among the reeds on sedges and swamp grasses: they fed partially submerged in the water, and the blobs of white on their shaggy coats acted as remarkably effective camouflage. I noted the great elongation of their hooves and the peculiar flexibility of their foot-joints: distinctive struc- tural characteristics which adapted them very well for this practice of swamp-grazing. The species of sitatunga to be found in the Okavango swamps is the most southern form of the three races, and was named after the famous explorer and hunter, Frederick Courteney Selous. As with the other two species the females are without horns, more conspicuously striped, and smaller than the males. When surprised, they can immerse themselves in the water and submerge entirely, with only the tip of the snout protruding above the surface. They often spend the heat of the day in the water. On dry land, their long hooves make them run a little clumsily.

Sometimes, again, I would come across impala, which would leap away to cover in a curiously erratic and unpredictable sort of way. If I disturbed a group of them – a stag, say, with the four or five wives of his harem, as they drank at a water- ing-place – they would often collide with one another in their efforts to spring away to safety, then apologising (or so it seemed) and moving off in those remarkable high bounds, even though there were no obstacles to clear. I tried to avoid disturbing and frightening animals wherever possible: it is not much to the credit of the human race that when we meet them most animals think it wisest to run.

Then, on one of these rides, I came across a troop of the Chobe chacma baboon – about twenty-five of them, strolling through the long grass on the west side of the river as I came riding up on the east side. They noticed me, and one large adult male acted as look-out, keeping me under constant observation, but without ceasing to grab bits of vegetation, bite at them, and wastefully cast most of them aside. He even ventured into the shallow waters of the riverside, yawning in apprehension at the unfamiliar sight of my binoculars. I saw some newly born infants, small and dark, riding on their mothers' backs and clinging on with the determination of jockeys. Some of the half-grown members of the troop – the bold adolescents – kept breaking their ranks in order to get a better look at me, but this was frowned upon by adult authority. Perhaps I was considered an unfit spectacle for the young to see, or perhaps there was an apprehension of danger. If one or two brave teenagers had crossed the river and fallen into my clutches, the troop would have been hard put to it to rescue them.

Baboons have their ways of asserting themselves against the human race, even so. One night Robert and I made a third – and still unsuccessful – attempt to catch a second springhare, and we went by foot to cause less disturbance and give less warning. On our empty-handed way back we were walking through a copse of acacias when we suddenly heard the shrill bark of a mature baboon overhead, and at the same moment a shower of faeces fell all about us, as thickly as cherry blossom in a springtime wind. We were not aware of sustaining any direct hit, or not at the time; but the smell of manure clung to us unpleasantly, and Robert found later that his bush-hat was liberally anointed. After that he made a great point of never forgetting to wear it when he went out in the bush at night. This was not the most gentlemanly way of repelling intruders, but it made great sense from the baboons' point of view, since it was likely to deter predators. In particular the elegant leopard – who is one of their chief enemies – would think twice before getting his velvety coat sullied in this way.

We only had two days now until the Smeetons and the District Commissioner were due to arrive, and we wanted to have plenty for them to see. So Robert made a slight alteration to the crate in which Chinky was to travel, thus converting it into a trap. We had seen a spoor in the light cotton soil some four miles to the north, and both Robert and June were convinced that it was the footprint of a cheetah. This was an exciting thought: I had found a fiancée for the Dublin-born lion back in the Jersey Zoo, and if I could find a mate for Paul, our cheetah, it would be a great triumph.

So we took this large heavy trap to a suitable site and covered its floor with soil, smoothing this across the threshold so as to make a continuous surface with the ground outside, and making sure that everything was firm and solidly mounted: we did not want any animal that might enter the trap to feel any suspicious movement underfoot, or to suspect that he was not still on ordinary ground. We also didn't want him to smell our human presence, and so we smothered the sides of the trap with wildebeest dung, then camouflaged the whole arrangement, except for the entrance, with branches. Robert fastened a piece of freshly killed meat to the far end of the trap and I crept inside to test the mechanism. Robert lubricated the grooves of the sliding door with fat and held it open with a small piece of metal, attaching this to a long piece of wire that ran along the top of the trap and round to the bait. Lying inside, I pulled at the meat gently, and at once the door slid down and closed with a thud. Robert then let me out: I was rather glad when he did. I might have been able to get out by myself: it's just possible that a chimpanzee could. But any large and less intelligent animal would be trapped securely.

Finally we trod in some wildebeest dung and spread that odour around the trap to mask our own, also brushing the ground with a branch. Then, leaving the trap carefully set, we returned to camp, with the intention of returning at first light next morning.

Excitement made sleep impossible for me that night. In the small hours of the morning, still wide awake, I rolled off my camp-bed and went over to Chinky's truck for a word with her: she too seemed to be restless, and I told her all about her travelling crate, and what we were now doing with it, and what we hoped to find in it in the morning. I also held forth on the charms of the Dubln-bred fiancé whom she would find at home. She seemed to be deeply interested in all this.

Just before dawn we were on our way, scattering several early foragers as we drove to the trap, swerving in this way and that to avoid the many potholes and the abundant vegetation. Robert, who was usually calm, appeared to be excited for once. We both felt sure that we would have caught something, even though my past experience hardly justified such optimism, and I dreamt gloatingly of my success. Would it be the longed-for cheetah? Or, failing that, a Delande's or bat-eared fox, or a specimen of the lynx-like caracal? It would be something marvellous, at all events.

In our impatience to find out we accelerated and covered the last quarter of a mile at high speed, scattering antelope and wild pig as we went on, still on, then past a final copse of mopane, and there it was – our trap, and yes, there was an animal inside it. We flung the doors open and tumbled out of the cab and saw – not a cheetah, but the wretched skulking form of a spotted hyena, just like the one I had seen with Captain Boathby at the Umtali Museum. It crouched at the far end of the trap, growling.

It looked a terrifyingly powerful animal, with jaws and teeth and muscles surpassing those of the larger carnivores. These hyenas can crack the leg bone of an ox as you or I would crack a match, and they can completely demolish the largest bones of the hippo and even of the elephant. Even so, while this one had damaged the sliding door of the trap in its efforts to get out, it had not bitten its way out. This said a good deal for the strength of the trap, and for Chinky's security in it during her voyage to England: it was a comfort in its way, making up in some degree for our disappointment.

It was a disappointment: I had no way of housing such an animal in my collection due to a hyena's strength, so we decided to write off the night's work and release it. We tied a rope to the top of the sliding door, brought it across the branch of a tree and across to the truck, so that we could open the trap from the safety of the cab. The hyena soon realised that it was free: it emerged, and its large form lumbered out and away, across the rough ground behind us, at a quite astonishing speed.

Unlike the striped hyena, the spotted hyena travel in large packs, and they eat on the spot rather than dragging the provisions to their lairs. They will attack a lone unarmed man at times; and they will always attack anything injured or small, a child or a small animal, domestic or otherwise, if not protected. They are unattractive beasts, both cowardly and aggressive, and in the worst sense of either word. Even so, I would like to have kept this one to show the Smeetons when they came, if only there had been another crate suitable for keeping it in: those bloodcurdling howls and growls and barks, so often ending with insane laughter, would have combined with Chinky's very different music to provide a fine orchestral accompaniment to our visitors' stay.

Our Batawana guide now came once again to give me aid and comfort in my hour of tribulation: for the rest of the morning, he showed me how to make and set small grass nooses, so as to catch such birds as might run through the thickets nearby. By sundown I had thus caught five red-billed francolin: this is a small grey grouse-like bird with an impressive deep red beak. I had not seen this species in zoological collections previously, and as they seemed easy to catch I decided to take a good basketful home. They differ from some species of pheasants, to which they are related, by the fact that the two sexes are alike; but the cock francolin, like the cock pheasant, can be distinguished by the spurs on his red legs. Of the five that I had now captured, four were thus seen to be cocks: I decided to catch three more hens to make a balanced collection of four couples.

Our guide's primitive methods seemed to work. By contrast, the small wire trap that had been so successful in Rhodesia, with the slender mongoose at least, failed completely with the Okavango fauna. I would set it regularly: it was always sprung but never occupied. Apart from one springhare and Chinky and a tortoise or two, my local collection was mostly a bird collection. Just before the Smeetons came I augmented it with a couple of ducks. This happened while I was taking the crocodiles down to the river in their wire box so that they could have their daily sulk in the water: I saw, a whole family of waterfowl and gave chase at once, almost dropping the crocodiles in my excitement. The mother duck broke cover and ran off, followed by eight ducklings stumbling confusedly after her: the last two took the wrong turning and came up against an impenetrable tussock of grass, thus giving me time to come up to them and catch them, while twenty yards in front I could see their mother feigning injury in the hope of distracting my attention, ready to sacrifice herself for the sake of her babies. I apologised to the crocodiles, took my ducklings back and put them into one of the baskets: within an hour they were accepting my offered pellets of broiler mash, mealie-meal, and munga seed, swilling this tasty food down with gulps of water.

I searched through my reference books to identify the species, but all the illustrations were of birds in adult plumage. I had seen the parents, but only briefly, since my mind was concentrated on the ducklings: I hadn't yet learned the importance of developing a photographic memory for wildlife, which is often seen for the shortest of moments and then not again.

This episode with the ducklings distracted me from something of the utmost importance – the importance of appearing smart and regimental when we had distinguished guests. So I embarked upon a quick shave; but just as I was dipping my safety-razor into a canvas basin of lukewarm water I heard the distinctive sound of a diesel engine, making heavy weather of the rough ground to the south-east of us. I shaved as hurriedly as I could, but it wasn't possible: before I had sorted myself out to receive company, a truck drove up alongside the DUKW and out stepped the District Commissioner and his wife, splendidly dressed and majestic in their bearing, every inch of them making it clear that they represented the British Crown in this part of colonial Africa. So I rubbed the remaining soap off my face and tried to rise to the occasion. Behind them, I saw two tall and youthful figures which were obviously Miles and Beryl Smeeton: even before we were introduced, I could sense their friendliness and their keen interest in everything they saw. After them the DC's guide emerged from the truck, and finally the total answer to the prayers of any young man who was ever in wild lonely places – two blonde girls, who at once descended upon the spaniels to envelop them in affection.

Robert and June handled the occasion with bush-camp informality but also with full observance of true British conventions. They made tea, and they also produced a tin of assorted biscuits that had often been discussed and hesitated over but not actually broached. Tea and sweet biscuits! We might have been in the cathedral close at Barchester.

Almost at once we were plunged into business by the taller of the two blonde girls, who turned out to be Clio, the Smeetons' only daughter. 'Come on,' she said, 'we're dying to see what you've collected!' So I thought quickly, and asked Robert to introduce the visitors to Chinky, our prize specimen, while I darted backstage to take a very necessary precaution. I went and terrified the vultures with loud noises and gestures. If there was going to be any regurgitation I thought it had better take place before these distinguished and sensitive guests arrived, rather than in their presence.

The animals performed well. Chinky enacted her fondness for Robert as fully as any theatrical producer could desire: she played patty-paw with him and licked his arms and face most impressively. Then Timmy staged a dramatic entrance from under the shade of the fig tree, scattered the brown hens, and took a nearly successful swipe at the terrified Henry. Thus both sides of lion character were displayed: the kittenish and affectionate, and the wild and predatory. 'You'd better watch Timmy when you're walking about camp – he's a little boisterous at times, and likes to grab people by the ankles': Robert uttered this warning quite seriously, but the

DC's wife seemed to take it completely in her stride. As for the crocodiles, they refused to move an inch: they looked exactly as they would if dead and stuffed. I explained that they were very much alive, and were in fact taken down to the river daily. They had not eaten any of the food that I had offered, but they had probably captured such small fish as swam foolishly into their cage when it was immersed.

The party now approached the row of vultures' cages, from downward as it happened, and just as a gust of warm air seemed to whirl around the cages and gather up all the scattered odour and roll it all into a ball and fling it at our visitors' nostrils. The DC responded in the highest traditions of Empire by making no response whatever: I did notice, though, that his moustache wilted as though sprayed with a powerful corrosive. His poor wife gasped, but soon rallied; and the Smeetons lived up to their reputation by pressing on, walking enthusiastically up to the origins of this appalling smell undeterred. Robert made hasty apologies for our odorous friends: they were not used to so many people approaching them at once, he said. And in fact they did not behave too badly: at least, thanks to my wise foresight, none of them regurgitated during this official inspection. I showed them off proudly: the eared vulture to begin with, whom we called Paris, then such lesser birds as the tawny eagle, the marabous, and the minor vultures.

We now came to the two ducklings that I had captured so recently, and the DC – having recovered from the gas attack – was able to identify them as members of the comb or knob-nosed species of duck. If either of them was a drake, he explained, he would develop a comb on the base of the upper mandible. They are quite plentiful in the Okavango, though he hadn't seen such young specimens for a long time.

I then showed off my red-billed francolin, and one of them nearly escaped: it had wriggled between the lid of the basket and the protective hessian lining, and flew up as soon as the lid was opened. I moved as smartly and effectively as any wicket keeper, and fielded it securely before it had taken more than one flap of the wings. There it was in my hands, its red beak gaping at our visitors. The DC's wife commented that francolins are very good to eat: an approach to wildlife that was not quite my own.

The tortoises came next: Clio picked up Albert and nearly dropped him, thus alarming him so seriously that he withdrew into his shell and raised the drawbridge and quite refused to be sociable. He thus gave a false impression of himself. For the last few days he and I had become very friendly: perhaps he thought that since I was so obviously a friend of those fearsome lions, it would be as well for him to keep on the right side of me.

The sun went down, the pale stillness of the brief tropical dusk came upon us, and the diurnal part of the local wildlife settled down just as the nocturnal part woke up: the camp fire crackled briskly, its noise blending in with that of the frogs and toads in the swamps nearby, its heat and glare keeping the mosquitoes away. All at once, Fig Tree Camp took on a different atmosphere. From a cellar deep in the bowels of the DUKW, Robert and June brought up an assortment of bottles, and soon we were sipping aperitifs from antique glasses. We even changed for dinner, feeling that the occasion warranted a special turn-out: that is to say, the men put on ties or silk scarves. In respect of manners, food, drink, and conversation, we ceased to be pioneers in the wild and became a weekend party in an English country house. But when the meal had come to a leisured end with coffee, the liqueur brandy came out, to warm and loosen our tongues and direct our conversation back to the one subject that was in all minds, the one question that was responsible for our being here – the subject of animal conservation.

There were several different points of view. Like so many naturalists before him, Robert had approached this subject by way of an original passion for big-game hunting. He had shot in Tanganyika, Rhodesia, and Mozambique, but now his chief concern was for the conservation of wildlife here in the Okavango. It was not that he had suddenly revolted against all killing of animals: in one sense he was still a hunter at heart, as became obvious when one saw him on the trail. It is one thing to kill for the pot. But it is quite another thing to stand by while the unbelievably rich fauna of Africa are systematically and irreplaceably destroyed with further unforeseeable consequences; and Robert was determined that at least this large inland delta of the Okavango should be saved from the greedy attentions of the safari firms, which were already seeking fresh killing-grounds for their rich clients.

June saw the question through the eyes of a journalist, and perhaps more emotionally, especially when she was involved in direct contact with the animals concerned. The steel gin-traps that were on sale in some of the trading stores near Maun infuriated her: whenever she saw one, she had visions of one of her beloved Bambis getting his legs caught and mangled in the jaws of such a trap and then dying slowly in terrible pain. I was with her in the Okavango for nine weeks, and during the whole of that time she was pounding away at her typewriter as though possessed, working without pause at the propaganda that was necessary if cruel traps were to be outlawed and if proper game reserves were to be established, safe from human exploitation.

The DC was a colonial administrator of the old school, scrupulously fair, wholly dedicated to the task of doing what he thought best for everybody and everything in the territory. N'gamiland was heavily subsidised, like the rest of the country, and it needed every penny it could get hold of: shooting licenses were a most useful form of revenue, and although little had come in so far – mostly from a trickle of South African hunters – there was promise of a great deal more. These safari firms in East Africa were deeply interested; the sporting concessions they sought would bring great wealth to the area; they were even proposing to improve the airstrip at Maun at their own expense for their customers' sake, but inevitably to the advantage of communications generally. This would benefit the European administration and people, and the authorities and tribesmen of the Batawana as well. Given the nature of his responsibilities, the DC was bound to take these considerations into account. But he recognised the importance of conserving the territory's wildlife, and suggested that this could best be done by restricting the number of licenses to be issued. With this approach to the matter, his wife was in wholehearted agreement.

Miles Smeeton had been a devotee of field sports for as long as he could remember, and fox hunting, tiger shooting and pig sticking had been his favourite pastimes when he was stationed in India. The more cunning the fox, the longer run it gave, the more elusive the tiger, the more ferocious the cornered wild boar, the better Miles was pleased with the hunt. But he saw the other side of the matter too. In the course of their travels, he and Beryl had seen the consequences of indiscriminate slaughter: at the very least it was necessary that a close season should be strictly observed, so that the game would be able to breed in peace, and if some area like the Okavango could be set aside as a reserve, so much the better. They would do everything in their power to support such a scheme.

It was a sound scheme. N'gamiland was an area large enough to support the game independently, without its having to move outside upon occasion for food and water, as with the Serengeti Reserve in Tanganyika. Safaris could continue, though with camera instead of gun; and scientific game-cropping could provide protein food for the indigenous population in those areas where the tsetse fly made it impossible to keep domestic cattle. Trapping for skins could and should be outlawed.

And so we talked on, over the coffee and brandy, trying always to make the DC fully aware of the urgency of the matter, until we were interrupted by a sudden clap of thunder. We felt that we had got somewhere. But the DC, being a practical administrator, was plainly worried by the obvious and inescapable question – who was going to pay? Robert and June had made a practical start, launching the whole idea of a game reserve and a N'gamiland Fauna Preservation Society; they had met with some success, but the money was still to be found. It was less than the cost of a single one of the jumbo jets that most modern nations seem to buy so freely.

The camp fire sank down to a hot glow, and we thought of bed. But sleep was not very attractive to us: we were too much taken up with this dream of a game reserve, and, long after the others had retired for the night, Robert and I sat up over the dying fire, dreaming and planning and hoping on lines which – as the night drew on – became less and less realistic.

But it was, and remains, a good dream.

CHAPTER 9

By Truck, Train and Plane

ON Easter Monday the DC and his wife left us, possibly to take part in the holiday festivities of their administration. But the Smeetons stayed with us at Fig Tree Camp for the last few days of our stay there, and soon came to share our absorption with the animal kingdom, both inside the cages and in the country around.

The two girls were extremely helpful in the daily tasks of looking after the animals: their nimble fingers were particularly good at a task which now became necessary: the weaving of reeds through the walls of various cages, so as to provide padding for the journey south. Their devotion to the animals was extreme, and it wouldn't have surprised me to find the vultures and marabous with their talons manicured and their beaks polished.

By now there was an end of term feeling in the air. John had discarded his previous gloom and now wore a water-melon smile constantly, aware that he would be going home soon. We set about our preparations. First of all we gathered up the dry branches with which we had built a kind of laager around our camp, and piled them all up to make a huge bonfire: it burned wonderfully, its great flames seeming almost to lick up to cloud level. Then there was the question of garbage. We wanted to leave the site as we had found it; so we thought it wise to dig a very deep trench and bury all our miscellaneous refuse beyond the reach of any inquisitive hyena. Shallow burying would not suffice: with our strong feelings about conservation, we did not want to feel responsible for the ugliness that would follow if our waste and mess were to be dug up and scattered around.

During our last night at the camp Chinky gave a last performance of her damsel in distress routine, but if the local lions heard it, they were not fooled by it: she was obviously some kind of collaborator or traitor. We rose an hour before dawn so as to make a daybreak start. We must have looked like a travelling circus or a gipsy encampment on the move. The DUKW was piled high with equipment and with vulture-cages, these being arranged to face outwards as a precaution in the event of regurgitation. June's diesel truck accommodated the bulk of the smaller cages, some inside and some on top. Chinky's truck had the aluminium dinghy strapped on top of it as before, and she herself lay in her reed-upholstered quarters in great state and spaciousness. Miles Smeeton travelled with Robert in the DUKW, Beryl Smeeton with June in the diesel, and the two girls – each with a spaniel on her lap – squeezed into the cab of Chinky's truck, leaving very little room indeed for the poor suffering driver, who was (of course) myself.

The first light of morning was just making the dew sparkle as we moved away from the fig trees in procession, grinding slowly forward to the place where we would be able to ford the Kwaai and thus reach its southern bank. Thereafter it was quite easy for us to retrace our steps southwards: even after six weeks the deep tracks made by the DUKW on our way north could be seen plainly, as could also the occasional branch that we had broken in our passage that was still hanging by the roadside. We had to keep to the old track, though certain short cuts were available and had in fact been used by the DC and his guide: these would have shortened the mileage, but were so rough that they would have seriously slowed us up. Even on the established track we were often reduced to a walking pace by the absolute necessity of not disturbing my collection too much.

I felt a good deal of anxiety about how easily all these

animals and birds would adapt to the traveller's life: they had a long journey ahead of them. So when we stopped for the night, I scrutinised their response to the idea of food. Chinky, Timmy, and Albert accepted food gladly, but the birds and the crocodiles and the springhare rejected with total finality the dainties that we offered. This worried me. But water was the main necessity, and I filled all the drinking troughs in all the cages from the supply kept in the DUKW: naturally enough, the rough journey had emptied them all, splashing water around in a way which only the crocodiles seemed to appreciate.

Another early start enabled us to reach the basecamp by the Thamalakane in the late afternoon of the second day of our travelling. Three hours later the whole collection had been offloaded: I conducted a minute inspection and found them all in as good condition as before, with the exception of Albert, who had once again been dropped by Clio.

I now had to wait five days until the Riley's Transport truck would take me and my collection to the nearest railhead in Francistown. I could not leave at once and on my own in the old three-quarter-ton pick-up: it was not nearly big enough, and I would have to sell it for whatever it would fetch. Meanwhile there was plenty to be done: in particular, there were permits to be obtained before I could take my collection out of the country. I also hoped that I might be able to get some more animals, and of course there was the feeding of the ones I had already. In all these matters I was helped wonderfully by John and the two girls.

It seemed that the DC was taking a great interest in my collection and talking about it in many quarters; and so I came to hear of the possibility of a second ostrich, a mate for the one already promised by the Greek trader at Sehitwa. This second specimen was owned by a member of the South African weather service, which had a station on the outskirts of Maun: it had reached the age of starting to be pernickety about people, of being friendly with some and aggressive towards others. It lived in the high fenced enclosure of the weather station and took a poor view of the meteorological staff, so that they could not get to work without being chased and attacked in a definitely dangerous way. To this situation I was the heaven-sent answer.

Miles Smeeton, Robert and I drove over to the weather station to size up this ostrich, so that a travelling-crate could be made for it. As we approached the nine-foot wire of the compound, it came strutting up and peering at us defiantly, as though daring us to come inside. It was about five feet tall and still carried its brown juvenile plumage; its large eyes were overhung with exaggeratedly long eyelashes, as worn by the more seductive type of cabaret artist. Its neck was like a pipe cleaner, its body was like a powder puff, its bony legs were like stilts, and its feet were murderous: when an ostrich attacks, it raises one leg and then strikes down, often disembowelling the enemy with the sword-like middle toe. If we made a crate for this one, it would need to be a small crate, in which it would be forced to crouch and would be prevented therefore from striking that kind of blow. It would also need to be well padded. As for the problem of how to get the dangerous bird into the crate . . . well, we would deal with that one when we came to it. I made up my mind, spoke to the ostrich's owner by field telephone – I didn't want to go into that enclosure unnecessarily – and said that I would be back that afternoon to collect it.

After lunch John and I cut some branches and set about making frames, covering them with wire-netting, and assembling them into a cage. It stood about 4 ft high, with an 18 in open-roofed extension on top, a kind of attic or penthouse for the ostrich's head. The sides were well padded with grass and hessian, and the floor was reinforced so as to carry the full weight of the bird when lifted.

We had a cup of tea, recruited a definitely unwilling John, and went back to the weather station. The ostrich greeted us as before, but the field telephone was silent. So we shouted loud and long, through the wire and across the enclosure and towards the neat white bungalow that stood there beneath its

weather masts and wireless masts. Eventually two beefy rugger
types appeared on the verandah, and we debated the problem
in bellows. I was very reluctant to run the gauntlet across the
enclosure to the bungalow: I didn't know yet whether the
ostrich would treat me as friend or enemy, and at this stage
of my collecting trip it would cause great difficulty if I were
to be laid up, even by some injury much slighter than an
ostrich can inflict when it tries. From the bird's truculent
manner it seemed certain that if we all went in, it would go
for at least one of us. What could we do?

The problem was solved for us by one of the two weather
men: he seemed to be less popular with the ostrich than the
other, who was its owner, and he ran down and attracted the
bird's attention and then ran from it into a small outhouse.
The ostrich pursued him inside very angrily, and he escaped
through the window of the outhouse just in time, and just
as the owner came dashing up and slammed the door from
the outside. We all breathed a little more freely, but the task
of getting the bird into its cage remained. The compound gate
was opened and we all drove in; then we took the cage down,
opened it at one end and located it as close as possible to the
door of the shed. Then we flung that door open and at once
clapped the cage firmly to the doorway: the ostrich was out
at once like a rocket, hitting the padded far end so violently
that he nearly knocked the whole thing over. We managed to
steady it and close the opened end, thus securing an ostrich
that now seemed perplexed rather than angry; but its feelings
were still strong, as John discovered when he forgot for a
moment that it was able to stick its head out through the open
end of its penthouse roof. One of his fingers sustained a nasty
peck; and from that moment on he had a healthy respect for
the ostrich, regarding it as yet another creature that was best
avoided.

We now asked him to make another ostrich cage, similar
to the one which had succeeded so well; and next morning,
after all the livestock had been looked after, Robert, Miles
Smeeton, the girls and I set out for Sehitwa to repeat the opera-

tion. Robert negotiated the fifty-odd miles of sand-track road in record time, and we soon jumped down on to the hard cracked mud in front of the Greek trader's store. The trader himself was nowhere to be found: his numerous children were there in quantity, but they refused to go and find their father, much preferring to stand there and feast their eyes on the amazing sight of us. Eventually the Greek did turn up, and dashed our hopes by saying that he'd changed his mind. The ostrich kept his poultry safe at night, and he didn't want to part with it.

Robert therefore embarked upon the diplomacy at which he excelled. We had made tremendous efforts, he explained, to find a mate for his ostrich, and now we had one. The trader seemed unimpressed. Moreover (Robert went on) we had achieved this through the good offices of the District Commissioner, who very much wanted my enterprise to succeed. This mention of authority did the trick at once: the trader was all smiles and helpfulness at once, and we all set to work much as before. To clinch the matter, I told him a true story about how a lion had recently been disembowelled by an ostrich, and asked him whether he really understood the danger to which his children would soon be exposed if the bird grew just a little larger while still a member of his household. He took the point, which was a valid one, and by the time we had the ostrich crated successfully, he seemed very glad to see it go. His poultry would have to be protected in some other way.

Before we went I asked him what had happened to the young impala that we had seen on our last visit. His children answered by laughing and pointing down their throats.

Back at the basecamp June greeted me with the exciting news that the larger of my two wire traps had caught a young vervet monkey, and was I going to keep it? I went to look. There it was, running to and fro on the platform in the middle of the trap, quite unable to see why it couldn't get out and rejoin its family and friends. It was a remarkably pale specimen as compared with the much darker vervets that I had seen at Mwanza and in the Vumba Mountains. Its body was olive grey with black speckling, its arms and legs were slate grey, its underparts were snowy, it had a pale nose, a charcoal-pencilled moustache and a grey muzzle. It was, in fact, an excellent example of environmental adaptation. the relatively pale colouring served as first-class camouflage in this sandy veldt country, in which the darker specimens would have been much more conspicuous.

Only two days now remained to me in N'gamiland, and I went into Maun to send a cable listing the collection of animals for which I needed transit permits. Most of their names were unfamiliar to the post-office orderly, and it took him an arduous half-hour before my own list could be copied out in his own handwriting – something that was unaccountably necessary before the cable could be sent off to Francistown. The episode tried my patience somewhat, and when it was over I went across to the small hotel in Maun to have a sandwich and recover my wits and do some thinking. But while I sat at the bar pondering, the sandwich was suddenly snatched out of my hand from behind. I spun round, thinking that I had some kind of bar-room fight on my hands, and there on the next stool sat a long-haired baboon. I was furious, and tried to snatch my sandwich back, but hesitated when she flattened her ears and bared her teeth like an aggressive dog. I just had to sit there while she bobbed up and down on her stool and rammed my precious sandwich down her own undeserving throat. Then the barman returned and told me that she could very easily be bribed into eternal friendliness by gifts of food. I had lost a sandwich but gained a friend.

It turned out that she belonged to an African truck driver who worked for the tsetse-fly control department: he would cycle to work each morning from his kraal, with the baboon on his back like an Indian papoose. Until recently she had accompanied him on his working travels, riding with him in the cab of his truck, but now the authorities had forbidden this: on one occasion she had seen something that interested her on the other side, and had leapt across to get a better view, grabbing at the steering wheel as she went. The result was a sudden swerve, a collision with the concrete-like bulk of an ant-hill, and a few unproductive days in hospital for the damaged truck.

Forty minutes later, having lost my first sandwich to this baboon and shared my second with her (but on my own terms), I walked out of the bar leading her proudly on a string with the air of someone who owns a pedigree dog. In a moment of infatuation I had paid five pounds for her. But I couldn't regret this: she was irresistible.

This new acquisition meant that my cable was out of date, so I went back to the post office to send another. But I found the orderly still puzzling over the first, apparently daunted by the task of sending it; so I added the name of my new girl friend to the list and stood over him until he had actually sent it.

Back at camp I made introductions all round, and then tied the baboon to a tree, using a rope which I fastened to a collar, this going round her thin waist rather than her neck. I then checked up on all residents. Both of my ostriches had taken well to their diet of fruit and vegetables: they had their heads out of their penthouse windows and were eyeing each other meaningfully. Maunensis, the vervet monkey, was eating particularly well, plainly enjoying a diet more varied than he had ever known in the wild. My only trouble was the loss of my Bechuanaland gerbil. I wanted to transfer him from his large cage to a smaller travelling-box; I couldn't find him, and ruffled through a big pile of his food in case he might be hiding beneath it. Finding nothing I looked up, and was just in time to see him leap out from behind the cage door and make a dash for freedom, in just the direction of the place where I had found him seven weeks earlier. I grabbed at him wildly and unsuccessfully: he would soon be at home. What travellers' tales he would have to tell his cronies! How unlikely they would be to believe him!

This loss was counterbalanced by the acquisition of three green tree squirrels in the smaller wire trap. I soon had them in exceptionally well-padded boxes: the other squirrels had damaged their heads on the wire, and I didn't want this to happen again. I thought of sending a further cable to bring the catalogue up to date, but my patience was not sufficient: these squirrels would have to travel as contraband.

On my last afternoon I had calls to make. First I went and paid my respects to Mahumahiti Moremi, and thanked her for allowing me to make an animal collection within her realm. I gave her my list, which she read through rather as though it was a menu, selecting one or two animals at random for gracious comment and question. Then one of her entourage broke into our conversation with the bare words 'Twelve pounds!' I took this to be the assessment of the tribal levy due on my collection, and I paid it over to the Queen Regent's treasurer without comment upon its somewhat arbitrary character. Then I shook hands with her and backed out of the room, so as not to turn my back on her: this I took to be the correct protocol for royal occasions. The effect was rather spoiled when I tripped over a dog.

My next call was on the European administration. The Veterinary Department gave me the documents that were necessary to take live animals out of N'gamiland to Francistown: there I would need to get a further veterinary permit before I moved them to the Rhodesian border. The DC's office stamped my collecting permit with a very impressive blue and red stamp, filled out an export permit in triplicate, copied the details from my passport into a visitors' book, and finally handed all these assorted documents to me in a big brown envelope that was boldly printed with the words ON HER MAJESTY'S SERVICE – BRITISH BECHUANALAND PROTEC-TORATE, so as to leave one in no doubt at all.

On my way back to camp I collected Miles Smeeton from the post office and we called in on the Calvers to pick up my spur-winged geese. The flower bed that had once been ravaged by the aardvark was now a mass of lovely blossom, and the geese had grown prodigiously. We carried the basket into their enclosure, and Miles and I set about catching them. It should have been easy: at least they couldn't fly away, since the primaries of their wings had been clipped. But they evaded us with surprising agility, until Miles lost patience and flung himself upon the gander in a high-speed rugger tackle, regardless of his own cleanliness. I should have shown such decisiveness myself, and I felt guilty when I saw the horrible mess that now covered his bush-shirt and trousers. But at least the goose was now easy to catch: she heard the indignant squawkings of her husband in the basket, came in wifely manner to help him, and was in our hands.

By now Robert had transferred Chinky to her travelling-cage. It had been well cleaned out previously, purged of its unseemly odours of wildebeest dung and hyena capture: she lay in it quite contentedly, stretched out on her mattress of freshly cut reeds, but her eyes were narrower than usual, and she kept vigilant watch upon the movements of June and Robert, being obviously aware that the immediate future was going to be different and unsettling. There was emotional stress on their side too: Chinky meant a lot to them, and would leave a painful gap in their lives when I took her away.

Last-minute visitors started to come: the Calvers, the DC and his wife, and a few others, all anxious to wish me well for a safe journey, while at the same time satisfying their curiosity. I acted as their host and guide as well as I could, but my attention was taken up by a hundred small adjustments to the cages and the other arrangements, and also by the necessity of giving the animals a big feed before the journey started. When it began it might well unsettle some of them and put them off their food: I wanted them to be well fattened up against this possibility. The tasks were small but endless in ways that can hardly be imagined unless you have had charge of animals, or perhaps of small children in quantity: the two girls helped most cheerfully, being motivated by their natural love of all animals, and John helped as well, with equal vigour but with different motivation. He wanted things to go smoothly so that he could get home quickly.

It was our last night. The guests had all gone, and we sat

back in camp chairs, our tasks accomplished for the moment, to enjoy one of Robert's rare and splendid curries. He really put himself out on this occasion, and produced a masterpiece to warm the stomach and comfort the soul. The night was chilly, but we had a good fire to warm us as we sat back in the verandah of our tent and looked down across the sloping ground to the Thamalakane. Around us, strange shapes loomed up in the firelight: the hessian-cloaked cages of the vultures and marabous on our right; the four baskets of water fowl and francolin by the water's edge; the cage of the vervet monkeys; the boxes of the crocodiles, the springhare, and the tortoises; and in the midst of all, the form of my friend the baboon, looking like a sentry who has fallen asleep at his post. It was as though we were all waiting for old father Noah to come and let us on board the ark.

The stars circled slowly and we talked beneath them – of my hope of returning to the Okavango some day, and of Robert and June's hope of establishing a game reserve there, so that for years to come other people would enjoy the privilege which had meant so much to me recently: that of seeing animals safe and unmolested in their natural setting. And as we talked I worked through the final stages of a task that had occupied me off and on all through my visit: the task of grooming the spaniels, of getting the tangles and the matted lumps out of their coats and ears. Now, at this last moment, I finished the job; but small thanks did I get from them.

The morning of departure came. The Riley's Transport truck was supposed to arrive at our camp between eight and nine: by the standards locally prevailing, we had to see great punctuality in its actual arrival at about ten fifteen. The driver appeared to me to be in no fit state to drive. But there was no alternative, and I embarked on the big task of loading.

This was complex. Each cage had to be accessible, of course, so that I could keep the animals fed and watered throughout the fifteen-hour journey; furthermore, it was important not to put any predator next to a possible victim. The four stony eyes of the crocodiles could not be allowed to frighten the already agitated Maun squirrels; the long coils of my python must be kept well away from the terrified and crouching springhare. Chinky's cage was located about half way along the right-hand side, and the two ostriches were put against it on the opposite side. The vulture cages were arranged in a row on top of some provisions, with the marabous alongside: I arranged my own sleeping-bag by the sliding door of Chinky's cage, just in case, with the waterfowl baskets opposite. As for the baboon, I tethered her at the back of the truck, just out of grabbing distance of any food or damageable cage: she would best enjoy the journey there, I thought, while also keeping guard if I had to leave the truck at any of the numerous stops between Maun and Francistown.

John's face shone like the morning sun as he said goodbye to his friends and got into the cab of the truck a good half hour before our take-off time. He wasn't going to risk being left behind. As for Robert and June, they climbed down slowly and reluctantly, after making their almost tearful farewells to Chinky. She was now my sole responsibility, and I was very glad that she liked and trusted me. Had any animal-gathering expedition to southern Africa ever come out with a more endearing and remarkable specimen?

Clumsily, with a genuine lump in my throat, I expressed my grateful farewells to Robert and June. They had been the best and most considerate of hosts. I was anxious to get my collection home; but I was also very sorry to leave them, and to part from a region and a style of life that I had grown to love.

But all things come to an end, and moments of departure are suddenly upon us. The green canvas awning was tied down on both sides, leaving the front and back open for ventilation, and the engine of the truck shuddered into noisy life. One of the marabous immediately and messily regurgitated its breakfast. Then, as Robin and June waved and as the baboon barked a farewell, we lurched forward and drove out of camp.

We crossed the creaking timbers of the Maun bridge, and I gazed for the last time upon the clear cool waters of the Thamalakane, the forests of reeds, the swamps of the Okavango. Then the truck gathered speed and away we went, bouncing over the rough road to the eastern boundary of N'gamiland, and then on through Bushman Pits, Kanye, Oudiakwe, and Nata, towards our destination of Francistown. At sundown the truck stopped, and we gladly accepted the invitation of the driver and his mate that we should join them in an evening meal; I took this opportunity to look after my charges. I replenished the seeds and water of the waterfowl and the francolin, which were duly grateful; I cut up some water melon and bananas and figs and fed them to the hungry ostriches; I raised Chinky's slide and gave her some fresh water, which she lapped up and then licked my arm with her rough tongue. I knew perfectly well that the marabou storks, the vultures, the tawny eagle, the crocodiles, and the python would be in no mood for eating. But Albert obliged me by sampling some lettuce and a slice of water melon that had been rejected by the smaller ostrich; and the Maun squirrels disentangled themselves from one another and from their connubial bed, and came forward to drink some water and nibble at some figs, their tails twitching in apprehension meanwhile. My friend Maunensis bobbed up and down at me while I was placing fruit in his cage, and then ate it all like a hungry soldier.

As for my new baboon – but she needed to have a name, she couldn't be just 'my baboon' for ever. I had thought of this before I left camp; and I had suggested to Clio Smeeton that in view of her gallant service and her devotion to duty, she might have this animal named after her. Clio agreed with enthusiasm, recognising this for the honour that it was: how many English girls can claim to have had baboons named after them?

I can therefore say that having checked the rest of my collection, I untied Clio from the back of the truck and took her along the sandy track so that both of us could have a little exercise. She led me a fine dance, ending up at a pool of stagnant water which she insisted upon sampling.

Then we journeyed on through the night, very much as

I had come, but in greater comfort and with less cramp. My mind was far too active for sleep, so I stayed alongside Chinky's cage, loving her through its structure, and meditating upon the past life of each of these animals and also upon the future that was in store for them. Freedom and danger then, captivity and safety now: it raised some thorny questions of the ethical sort, and about these (not for the first time) I brooded.

As the night and the bouncy journey continued, I became more and more afflicted by the continual sandstorm that blew in from the front; and I tried to close the canvas, to reduce its impact, but with doubtful success. My animals, however, seemed all right. Exhausted, the ostriches and the marabous had crouched down on their haunches and gone to sleep; by the light of my torch I could see the vultures gripping their perches tightly with their immensely powerful talons, and thus steadying themselves against the joltings of the truck. My dear Chinky had pillowed her great head down on to her broad paws, but she was not asleep: she kept opening her large friendly eyes, to check up on me and make sure she had not been deserted.

In the very early morning there was a completely unexplained hold-up of a whole hour, in some completely unidentifiable place. Despite this we drew up in the goods yard of the station at Francistown almost exactly at the scheduled time. They knew about me and were ready. The Afrikaans station master had allocated us a spacious closed-in wagon, and this was parked all ready in a siding, and he issued us with two fourth-class tickets so that John and I could travel in this wagon with the animals. We now faced the task of transferring them from the truck to the wagon, and a large crowd assembled to enjoy this spectacle, with many a helpful but noisy comment which did little to soothe my collection. I was fretful with lack of sleep, and I was glad to speak up on their behalf and call for a little peace, but without much effect: soon I felt an ignoble temptation to set Chinky upon them as a sobering influence.

This would hardly do, but Clio managed at least to keep them at a distance.

We completed the transfer, and I left John and Clio to guard the wagon, making it clear that nobody except the station master was to be admitted. I had watered and fed my stock, and I now wandered off into the dry heat of Francistown – it was well into the nineties – in search of provisions and fresh permits.

I found a fine old confusion. The Veterinary Office had not received word from Salisbury to authorise the transit of my collection through Rhodesia; it was now after noon, and for the next two hours it would be impossible to phone Salisbury; I would therefore miss the mid-afternoon train that was supposed to be taking me and the animals northwards; the cable that I had sent from Maun some forty-eight hours previously had not arrived. So, in resignation, I bought some fresh fruit and some meat and returned heavily burdened to the station.

There I found two somewhat bombastic Afrikaans policemen waiting for me; John had managed at least to keep them out of the wagon by saying that Clio was dangerous and quite uncontrollable. Thus thwarted they released their anger in a display of petty officialdom. They inspected my passport closely, also John's entry permit, disturbed all the animals by a pointless scrutiny, and then tipped out the contents of one of my cases on to the grubby floor of the truck. Sighing wearily, I produced receipts to show that I had paid tax, and permits to show that I was authorised to transport my collection. It was all very boring, but the story has a happy ending: one of these junior policemen was rash enough to put his hand where the older and fiercer ostrich could get at it, and was powerfully nipped, to my extreme gratification.

Thus the afternoon passed in the hopeless war against bureaucracy, and by night-time I had received the necessary authorisation to take my collection into Rhodesia, together with a fresh veterinary certificate from the authorities at

Francistown. The station master told me that a goods train would come and pick us up later on in the evening, at a time which could not be predicted, so that we would do well to remain on board the wagon. So we did, and eventually we felt a terrible jolt that knocked most of the birds off their perches. After that, however, things went much more smoothly; we were coupled on to the train and then proceeded in what seemed – by contrast with the previous night's travel – the most velvety and luxurious fashion, even though the train had to fight its way up the steep incline into Bulawayo.

The vultures celebrated their arrival in Rhodesia by greedily accepting some of the meat that I had bought in Francistown. Chinky was also willing to eat, provided that I cut it up and fed it to her by hand. She needed attention, she wanted to be looked after: the parting from Robert and June had been a shock that she could not have expected and could not now understand.

I kept the broad door of the truck permanently open, as there was no other ventilation. Whenever the train stopped in Matabeleland I would jump down alongside the track and pull up bunches of the yellow stringy grass to feed to the ostriches, gathering its roots as well for the springhare. Clio was housetrained and needed to be excercised at these whistle-stops for personal reasons: it must have provided an unusual spectacle for any onlookers when a baboon with a European in tow was to be seen jumping on to a goods wagon.

We arrived at Salisbury in the early hours of the morning, and our wagon was detached and shunted into a siding. There was nothing that I could do now until the city came to life, so I fell asleep by Chinky's side, my snores doubtlessly counter-pointing hers.

I woke up when the morning was well advanced, and secured from the Veterinary Department a permit to take my collection out to Glendale for the three days that remained before the Africargo flight to London upon which we were all booked. A transport company supplied me with a sufficiently large truck, and so we went forth on the familiar road to Douet Farm.

John was in his glory, and as we went past Mazoe Dam he took on the role of a returning and triumphant Caesar, waving to every African by the roadside, his cheeks blossoming with goodwill, his confidence expanding with every mile.

And so we came back to Douet, and to a tumultuous welcome: I quite expected the boss boy to come out and put a garland on John's head. It was good to see Robin and Pris again; they saved me from the throng and helped me to unload everything into the old tobacco barn, which still smelt slightly of hunting dog and jackal. Chinky had a private suite – the garage to be precise – and the tractor had to live outside for the time. The whole collection made a wonderful impression: Roselle fell in love with Maunensis above all, while James – bold as ever – decided that Chinky was for him.

Once again I had a problem of accommodation. For the spurwing geese, which had been seriously cramped in their basket, I took over one of the poultry pens. As for Clio, I tethered her to a tree in front of the farmhouse, so that she could perform her various tricks within sight of the children. But she interested other people too; and one day, while she was deeply engaged in inspecting the long coarse brown fur of her back, a crowd of Africans gathered and were soon laughing at her. She could not endure this mockery, and strained at her leash for revenge: this increased the laughter and made it more hostile, and she strained more violently, until by a happy chance the catch on her chain broke. The jeering became a collective shriek of terror, and the unkind crowd dispersed to the four winds: the worm had turned, the fox had bitten the hounds.

New acquisitions still came pouring in. The Smoelkes presented me with three leopard tortoises, which I was glad to have, though Albert was somewhat put out by this competition. Then, thanks to a news item about the departure of my Rhodesian collection, Robin had been contacted by a bird fancier in Livingstone, who wanted to know whether I would like to have a fish eagle and a martial eagle. He had accepted on my behalf. The fish eagle was the replica of the one that had foraged for food near the DC's house in Maun; with its white head and neck establishing its adult status, it looked thoroughly proud and arrogant. The martial eagle, with its magnificent crest, had been shot in the left wing by some trigger-happy European; a Mr Oxenham had rescued it and mended its wing as well as he could, and it now looked extremely healthy, though when it perched its left wing would hang slightly, the primary feathers not tucking up to the tail feathers as they should.

The weekend passed rapidly. The animals were all eating well, except for the crocodiles, which had renewed their hunger-strike. John and I basked in glory. He had acquired the reputation of a fearless hunter, and this was useful to me, since it meant that he worked very hard to live up to the prevailing image of himself. As for me, I was written up in the *Salisbury Press*, after a reporter's visit to Douet Farm, and I was given the undeserved titles of explorer and zoologist. In fact I was neither. But I was glad of this article, since it gave useful publicity to the conservation work of Robert and June in the Okavango, and also to the work of Gerald Durrell at the Jersey Wildlife Preservation Trust.

With the animals well rested and well fed, we departed for Salisbury for the last time, after brief but exceptional hospitality at the farm. As I drove past the wooded kopjes and the uncultivated part of the land, which was now pretty well devoid of animals. I thought how splendid it would be to liberate my collection in just such a place, in order to recolonise it – if only it would be safe from human persecution.

Chinky saw the broad waters of the Mazoe Dam, and perhaps thought that she was back in the Okavango. The ostriches fluttered their eyelashes at one another foolishly. Clio sat unhappily in an uncomfortable box: she was a seasoned traveller, familiar with trucks if not with aeroplanes, but the airline had insisted that she was not to be loose on the plane.

The Game Department gave me an export permit, and the Veterinary Department passed the whole collection as being free – as far as they could detect – from contagious diseases. As we passed down First Street in Salisbury, a press photographer took a picture of Chinky, which appeared in the evening paper with the caption 'Lion Roars in First Street!' In point of fact Chinky hadn't uttered a sound since we left the northern regions of the Okavango. Never mind: it made a nice fantasy for the readers, to think of a pride of lions invading the urban streets of Salisbury.

And so we came to Salisbury Airport, where I had great difficulty in controlling the porters, who swarmed like ants over the truck in their anxiety to see what was in these different cages. If they had been left to their own devices, most of the cages would have been hauled off the truck in any old fashion, upsidedown or sideways, to the great detriment of the occupants. I had to keep control. But at least we got the publicity. A television man brought a bloodshot eye up to the squint-sights of his camera and took a series of shots while the collection was being weighed, incessantly distracting me from the job with requests for a cheesy smile. And as I stood by Chinky's cage, a small boy came up and asked me for my autograph. But here I may have been sought out under a misapprehension: the British Lions rugby team had arrived in Rhodesia that very afternoon, with their mascot, and this boy may have supposed that I was one of them. I had no such glory.

Now it was time for the empty lorry to go back to Glendale, and this meant that I had to say goodbye to John, who was going back with it. This also was a parting which grieved me. Ours had been an odd relationship, more deep-rooted than it seemed, rather like the relationship between a school prefect and a fag. He seemed very cheerful and confident about his own future: with the money he had earned while he had been with me he proposed to seek out and buy a good hard-working wife. I told him that I would be coming back to Africa next year on a similar quest, and that he would be the first person I would wish to employ. He grasped my hand emotionally, and so we parted. What stories he would have to tell, back in the home kraal, of intrepid hunting and of ferocious animals boldly captured by himself!

The aircraft was a DC6 freighter; I was the only passenger, listed in the flight manifest as an animal attendant – yet another new title for me. I checked that all the cages were held firmly in place by the straps provided, and I blocked up a small hole in the wire door of Clio's cage: she had been busily at work enlarging it so as to get a better view around the aircraft. I had brought a good supply of tranquillisers to administer to Chinky if necessary, but she seemed very peaceful, and so I did not give her any, feeling that my own presence, close at hand, would soothe her better than any chemical. These tranquillisers are often very useful on a short-term basis, but when the effects wear off, the animal tends to be under worse stress than if it had received no medication at all. And we had a long journey: I had to take the long-term view.

The piston engines of the DC6 spluttered into life and were then run up and tested, to the astonishment of the passengers: the crocodiles tried to submerge in some non-existent water, and the ostriches stood petrified. Chinky lay flat on a mattress of wood-wool, her ears flickering; she was disorientated and bewildered by the alien noise, and her eyes were narrow and uneasy. I raised the sliding door of her cage slightly so that I could scratch her reassuringly under the chin. She seemed grateful for this, and lowered her head on to her paws, with my hand caught between them as I lay alongside her cage. It was in this position – which is not what stewardesses usually recommend – that I experienced the taxiing of the aircraft, the slow turning on to the runway, the roar of full power, and the swift rough acceleration of the take-off.

Soon we were at cruising height, and the engines settled down to a steady quiet roar. Chinky felt better now – after all, even the most experienced air traveller feels a shade nervous during the take-off and the initial climb – and she started to sandpaper my bare arm. We both took up more relaxed positions. Soon, in defiance of orders, I succumbed to Clio's entreaties and took her out of her travelling-box, so that she could inspect the tubular interior of the DC6. I kept her firmly under control by her waist-collar; she seemed beside herself with exitement when she happened to look out of a window and see the vast immensity of the land beneath her. It amazed me too, especially when I saw the snow-capped heights of Mount Kilimanjaro, gleaming in the sunshine like a diamond-studded snowball in a desert. The fact is that Clio enjoyed air travel, finding it much more exciting and spectacular than anything she had experienced in the cab of that tsetse fly control truck. I had the greatest difficulty in getting her back into her cage.

Our first landing was at Nairobi, where we took on board some further animal cargo, unconnected with myself. There were ten plywood boxes crammed full of Fischer's lovebirds, which abound on the slops of Mount Kenya: they had been netted and packed like sardines for shipment to a dealer in Holland. There were also two domestic dogs. One was an angry Scottish terrier who seemed most reluctant to leave the warmth of Africa for his own damp misty homeland: the other was a miniature pug, who yapped hysterically until silenced by a well-timed roar from Chinky. Clio put on her dog voice and barked a little at these newcomers, but received no reply. Perhaps they were petrified.

When we next landed, this time Khartoum, I noticed that the ostriches were running out of green food: they had been eating it greedily during the flight, and now there was none left. I descended from the aircraft and went across to the airport building, which was guarded by a real forest of bayonets. Through these I managed to see a civilian wearing the white smock and red fez of a waiter, and I got hold of him and ordered two dozen lettuces. After about twenty minutes he came out to the aircraft, escorted by a Sudanese soldier who was carrying his rifle in a distinctly threatening manner. I was given four cardboard cake-boxes. I opened one of them and found six small lettuce hearts, denuded of the more acceptable and nutritious outer leaves. I tried to explain that they were for my ostriches and not for myself, and that if this chap wanted me to pay his hefty bill he would have to find the outer leaves too. He didn't *want* to understand, and the soldier fidgeted with the trigger of his rifle in a more and more pointed way. So I stormed across the tarmac, pushing my way boldly past the soldiers, and found the kitchen, where I accosted someone who must have been either the manager or else the cook. Whoever he was, he pretended not to understand my perfectly simple request for the outer leaves of those lettuces to serve as ostrich food. It was almost as though he had never met such a requirement before. But as is often the case with foreigners, violent gesticulation did the trick; and soon I was back in the aircraft with a big polythene bag full of what I wanted. The ostriches were duly grateful, or greedy at least.

Here at Khartoum the heat was quite suffocating, though it was after dusk. I kept myself busy by watering the whole of my collection, dampening the waterfowl baskets continually, and even pouring water over the unresponding forms of the apparently mummified crocodiles. Chinky was restless now, and paced up and down fretfully: the ninety-minute stop seemed like half a day, and I was extremely glad when we took off again into the cloudless night sky.

We touched down at Malta in the early hours of the morning for the third refuelling and the second change of air-crew. The animals were all still in good shape, though Chinky became nervous once again as take-off approached, and insisted on being scratched and fondled and then upon holding my hand, just as when we first left Salisbury.

And so the great journey moved on to its ending, until we bumped down on to the runway at Heathrow and taxied to the terminal building. I was greeted there by a horde of officials who seemed to be much more interested in my collection than in their proper bureaucratic task of checking my documents.

I had meant to carry on to Jersey immediately. But my return happened to coincide with a lightening strike of airport engineers, so that all domestic flights were grounded. For three days my collection had to be accommodated at the RSPCA hostel at Heathrow, where every possible attention and comfort was provided for them.

Meanwhile there were the newsmen, and my story ends with them. I knew already that when I reached Jersey I would be met by a BBC television team, who were collecting film for one of Johnny Morris's children's programmes. They wanted to film Chinky's first meeting with her fiancé, the Dublin-born lion called Leo. Since this was now impossible because of the strike, they wanted to record her great friendliness towards human beings, which had already been the subject of a press release. So I was asked to demonstrate here in London.

This was a somewhat unnerving prospect. Chinky had not been out of a cage for nearly six months, long before my arrival in Bechuanaland. She had certainly shown many signs of goodwill and affection towards me, especially since parting from Robert and June, but this had only been a matter of holding my hands and washing my face while she was securely caged. I did not really know how she would behave when given the chance of some wider relationship; and after all, she was a lioness, not a kitten.

The time came for the filming to take place. She was released from her travelling cage into a large indoor den, where she looked larger than ever. The producer and the cameramen, from a safe place outside, gave me the signal that they were ready. Slowly, apprehensively. I put on a thick duffle coat by way of extra protection, and went in.

I need not have worried. Chinky sprang to her feet in obvious delight, curled her lips in a smile, gave forth a gentle cub-like roar, and jumped up to put her big paws on my shoulders, thus flattening me against a wall, and then joyfully sandpapering my cheeks with her tongue. I felt utterly smitten with guilt at having doubted her friendship, and I hugged and embraced her like the sweetheart that she was.

I had travelled many miles. But a man could journey over the whole of this wide world, meeting animals and men of every kind, and still never meet such a friend as she. I was lucky.

Postscript

FINANCIALLY, my African journey was a disaster, for I found that it was impossible to regard any animal as a piece of merchandise to sell to the highest bidder. But although I had lost in credit, I had been rewarded a thousand times over with a treasure chest of unforgettable animals and events, which perhaps not even money would be able to purchase in the future.

I considered that the essential prerequisite of sending an animal anywhere was to know that it was going to be looked after properly by a sympathetic establishment. Perhaps general collections are not now really justifiable, since if a species is to benefit from captivity, it must be represented in sufficient numbers to provide viable breeding units. By captive breeding and good management zoos and other organisations handling 'exotic' animals could be almost self-supporting, and would not have to keep drawing on the increasingly depleted wild populations. However, it is almost impossible to achieve this goal, unless sufficient numbers of the same species can be collected and imported at much the same time, so that compatible pairs will result in regular propagation. A number of animal species already owe their survival to the protection afforded them in a controlled environment.

Some of the animals I collected have been kept at the Jersey Zoo, although over the years some of them have been sent to other collections, to make way for more specific breeding programmes.

The Zoological Society of London accepted a pair of the red-billed francolin, the first of this species to be represented in the Society's collection: their presence was given a learned mention in both the Zoological Record and the Avicultural Magazine.

The Royal Zoological Society of Scotland maintained the pair of cape hunting dogs in a spacious rocky enclosure; whilst Chessington Zoo in Surrey looked after the black-backed jackal.

The Bristol, Clifton and West of England Zoological Society purchased Paris the eared vulture; whilst the North of England Zoological Society, at Chester, played host to a trio of the white-headed vultures.

Flamingo Park, in north Yorkshire, accepted the ostriches; and the Welsh Mountain Zoo, at Colwyn Bay, who were specialising in birds of prey, purchased the martial eagle.

After a six-year stay in Jersey Clio left the island to take up an appointment at the Marquess of Bath's Longleat Park, to become a founder member of the baboon colony, which was in close proximity to familiar lions. Clio was also honoured by Dr W. C. Osman Hill, who included a portrait photograph of her in the eighth volume of his renowned monograph on the anatomy and taxonomy of primates; thus ensuring that Clio's presence on this earth will be preserved for posterity as the representative of *Papio ursinus chobiensis*.

The black spur-wing geese now reside in the graceful parkland of the Château de Cleres, near Rouen, France, in the collection of the famous ornithologist Jean Delacour. A dead Maun squirrel, perhaps not as fortunate as the others, is preserved in the mammal room of the British Museum, representing the only specimen of the type species, *Peraxerus cepapi maunensis*.

The Jersey Wildlife Preservation Trust recorded the first captive breeding of the red-billed francolin, and some of the progeny have been exported to England, Holland, and the USA.

The serval cat Tammy has given birth to twenty-two kittens. Some of the young have been sent to Regent's Park and Whipsnade in England; Wassenaar Zoo in the Netherlands, and to the Rare Feline Center in Florida, USA. Recently she has become a grandmother twice over.

Maunensis, the Okavango vervet Monkey, matured into a fine male, and has now perhaps created a record amongst the vervet heritage by successfully siring nine young, five sons and four daughters, in the space of seven years. It is rumoured that he is soon to become a grandfather.

Chinky and I could hardly have thought more deeply about each other: the depth of our affection appeared to be unfathomable. Whenever she caught sight of me approaching her enclosure she would utter her 'wow' of greeting, and her golden form would trot effortlessly over to talk to me: much to my gratification and to the infuriation of her possessive mate. Almost a year after Chinky's arrival in Jersey it was established that she had been successfully mated by Leo. Letters flowed between the Okavango and Jersey with the same degree of intensity as if I had married Robert and June's daughter, and was about to become a parent at any moment. However, during the final stages of pregnancy, an internal virus suffocated the cubs, and before it was possible to save her life she died.

At the time of her death I realised that there could never be a replacement in the animal world for Chinky. She had become a part of my life and had taught me so much about the true understanding of animal friendship, and the realisation of how important it was to cultivate a mutual respect between man and beast – a relationship once achieved, impossible to surpass.

Appendix: The Animal Collection

2   European red foxes

24	Assorted frogs		1	African tawny eagle
2	Chameleon		1	Martial eagle
1	Bell's hinged tortoise		1	Fish eagle
3	Leopard tortoise		3	Marabou stork
1	Rock monitor		2	Southern ostrich
2	African crocodile		1	Chacma baboon
1	Mole snake		1	Okavango vervet monkey
3	Python		3	Maun squirrel
4	Hottentot teal		1	Cape pouched mouse
4	Red-billed teal		1	Rhodesia bush hare
2	Black spur-wing goose		1	Springhare
8	Red-billed francolin		1	African lion
2	White-backed vulture		1	Slender mongoose
3	White-headed vulture		2	Black-backed jackal
1	Eared or lappet-faced vulture		2	Serval cat
1	Yellow-billed kite		1	African wild cat
2	African goshawk		2	Cape hunting dog

SPECIMENS COLLECTED — RELEASED OR ESCAPED

1	Rock monitor*		3	Double snipe
Numerous	assorted frogs*		1	Giant kingfisher*
1	Leopard tortoise		1	Coucal
1	Striped skaapstekker*		1	Long-tailed starling
3	Red-billed francolin*		1	Bechuanaland gerbil*
3	White-backed vulture		3	Maun squirrels
1	Barn owl		3	Slender mongoose*
18	Blacksmith plover		1	Blotched genet
2	African skimmer		1	Spotted hyena
1	Avocet		*	Denotes escapees

Index